The Motif of Io
in Aeschylus' *Suppliants*

The Motif of Io in Aeschylus' *Suppliants*

Robert Duff Murray, Jr.

PRINCETON, NEW JERSEY
PRINCETON
UNIVERSITY PRESS · 1958

Copyright © 1958 by Princeton University Press
ALL RIGHTS RESERVED
L.C. Card 58-7128

Publication of this book has been aided
by the Whitney Darrow Publication Reserve Fund
and by the Ford Foundation program
to support publication, through university presses,
of works in the humanities and social sciences.

Printed in the United States of America
by Princeton University Press, Princeton, New Jersey

TO
I. S. M. AND J. S. M.

PREFACE

THIS brief study of Aeschylus' *Suppliants* is in no sense exhaustive. It offers an interpretation of the play, but does not pretend that the interpretation is definitive; I hope only that it may cast some small light on a rewarding approach to Aeschylean tragedy. My specific objective is to demonstrate that Aeschylus has woven around the theme of Io a web of imagery central to the meaning of the drama.

The legend of Io, which is familiar to the student of Greek literature, was old in the time of Aeschylus. Io was the daughter of an Argive king and a maiden of exceptional beauty. Her charms inevitably attracted the attention of Zeus and, equally unfailingly, the jealous eye of Hera; in turn, Zeus, that he might visit Io secure from his wife's anger, transformed the girl into the shape of a cow. Thus Io became an unwilling victim (in the true sacrificial sense), banished from her father's palace, metamorphosed from maiden to horned creature, deprived of form and birthright. This was but the beginning of her travail, for the suspicious Hera appointed many-eyed Argus to watch over her. The grotesque herdsman soon was slain by Hermes, the agent of Zeus, but was then transformed into a gadfly, which was to pursue the now tormented and maddened Io over the wastes of Asia. Finally, she reached Egypt and the Nile. Here Zeus, in an act of

Preface

release and procreation, restored her to human form. Thereafter, she gave birth to the bull deity Epaphus, god and ruler.

This primitive myth has little superficial relevance to the *Suppliants*, beyond the fact that the Danaids are the descendants of Io and Zeus, and appeal thereby to Zeus and Pelasgus for protection and asylum in Argos. Its inner and vital relevance is, however, immense, for the myth and its application uniquely illuminate the character of the Danaids, heighten the dramatic tensions, and unveil in marked measure the meanings intended by the dramatist. In brief, I shall try to show that the story of Io is treated by Aeschylus as a prefiguration of the experience of the Danaids, that the fifty maidens themselves are deeply aware of the relationship of their situation to that of Io, but misinterpret the true nature of that relationship, and that this misinterpretation decisively affects the tragic issues.

Although the *Suppliants* has received its full share of thorough scholarly scrutiny, I have made no attempt to discuss or refer to all existing interpretations and theories. My objective is only to examine the techniques by which Aeschylus integrates the motif of Io into his poetic structure, and to consider the manner in which his manipulation of the motif assists our interpretation of the tragedy. Most of my findings are based on independent study of the text of the play; for this reason, I have referred to other publications only to acknowledge indebtedness, to corroborate my conclusions, or to supply the reader with a general

Preface

picture of the state of critical opinion concerning contested points of interpretation.

I have adhered, in quotations and references, to the Oxford text of Gilbert Murray (2nd edition), and have called attention in the notes to my infrequent use of other readings. The translations (which aim for prosaic clarity) occasionally contain borrowings from H. W. Smyth's version in the Loeb Classical Library.

I am deeply indebted to all of my colleagues in the Department of Classics of Princeton University for their encouragement and assistance. In particular, I am grateful to Professor Antony E. Raubitschek for his challenging counsel and unflagging interest, and to Professor Francis R. B. Godolphin for his sympathetic criticism. I wish also to thank President Robert F. Goheen, Professor John V. A. Fine, Professor Lawrance R. Thompson, and Professor William Arrowsmith (now of the University of Texas) for their valuable suggestions.

R.D.M., Jr.

Princeton
January 1958

CONTENTS

I. Introduction	3
II. The Imagery of the *Suppliants*	18
III. The Aeschylean Io	46
IV. The Meaning of the Motif of Io	56
V. Hypermnestra and the Themes of the Trilogy	77
Appendix A: The Chronology of the *Suppliants* and the *Prometheus Bound*	88
Appendix B: Line 8 and the Motivation of the Danaids	98
Bibliography	103

The Motif of Io
in Aeschylus' *Suppliants*

I. Introduction

FEW GREEK TRAGEDIES confront the critic with more varied difficulties than the *Suppliants* of Aeschylus, and perhaps no other tragedy has been the subject of such diverse interpretation. A casual examination of the recent scholarship devoted to the play and its trilogy reveals that there is virtually no agreement concerning its principal theme, which, to list only a handful of opinions,[1] has been interpreted as (1) the struggle of the Danaids against marriage; (2) the formal establishment of the institution of matrimony and the concomitant change in the status of women; (3) the emancipation of women; (4) the question of the right of women to refuse forced marriage, and the establishment of the Thesmophoria; (5) the sanctity of marriage; (6) the question of exogamy versus endogamy; (7) the rights of the suppliant; (8) the conflict between divine custom and state law; (9) the conflict between human rights and the divine ordinance which is not yet fully expressed in human laws, customs and needs; (10) the will of Zeus, which brings harmony out of chaos.[2]

---

[1] The brief summaries that follow are, in most cases, oversimplifications. The full significance of several of the hypotheses referred to can be grasped only in context.

[2] These are, in order, the interpretations of (1) Ulrich Von Wilamowitz-Moellendorff, *Aischylos Interpretationen*; (2) George Thomson, *Aeschylus and Athens*; (3) A. Suesskand,

Introduction

The difficulties conducive to such diversity of opinion spring from several sources. A rather alarming portion of the text of the *Suppliants* is unusually obscure, often because of extreme corruption, and even in some cases because of seemingly intentional vagueness on the part of the dramatist. In dealing with such parts of the text, it is the task of the critic to re-examine carefully the manuscript readings, avoiding categorical acceptance of modern emendations which sometimes tend to obfuscate rather than illuminate. He must also beware of the pitfall into which not a few scholars have fallen, that of basing interpretative hypotheses on emendations of hopelessly corrupt passages.

A second and even more important factor working to obscure the meaning of the *Suppliants* is the almost total loss of the other two members of the trilogy; the critic would be in an analogous position if, possessing only the *Agamemnon*, he was faced with the necessity of reconstructing the *Oresteia* and analyzing the full significance of the *Agamemnon* itself. Intelligent and cautious conjecture, not certainty,

---

"Einfuhrung in die Hiketiden des Aeschylos," *Berliner Philologische Wochenschrift* 40 (1920), cols. 738-44 and 761-8; (4) D. S. Robertson, "The End of the Supplices Trilogy of Aeschylus," *Classical Review* 38 (1924), pp. 51-3; (5) Paul Mazon, *Eschyle*, pp. 3-11; (6) William Ridgeway, *The Origin of Tragedy*, p. 193; (7) J. Vürtheim, *Aischylos' Schutzflehende*; (8) Hans Bogner, *Der Tragische Gegensatz*, pp. 104-39; (9) Kurt Von Fritz, "Die Danaiden Trilogie des Aeschylus," *Philologus* 91 (1936), pp. 121-36 and 249-69; (10) J. T. Sheppard, "The First Scene of the Suppliants of Aeschylus," *Classical Quarterly* 5 (1911), pp. 220-9.

Introduction

is all that the scholar can properly hope to achieve given such a situation.

The *Suppliants*, which has come down to us in the Laurentian (Medicean) manuscript, evidently belonged to a tetralogy, of uncertain date, which included also the *Egyptians*, the *Danaids*, and the satyr-play *Amymone*.[3] The order of the three tragedies within the trilogy has been disputed, but the view that the *Suppliants* was the first play, the *Egyptians* second, and the *Danaids* third is now commonly accepted.[4] Fragments from the latter tragedies are scant: for the *Egyptians*, only one word is ascribable with any assurance;[5] rather more has been preserved of the *Danaids*, but even so, only one fragment (number 44) of this play warrants close attention in interpretation of the trilogy.

Confronted with the sparseness of evidence, the critic may reasonably inquire if the extant play may not be examined as an isolated, independent work of art. Of course it may, and profitably; it will not, however, yield up the full richness of its meaning, and such a study, if pursued without great care, may misread badly the intentions of the dramatist. The proper approach to the *Suppliants* is one which considers the play as a work of art accidentally detached from its fuller context, and to be regarded as meaningful only

[3] The titles appear in the catalogue of the Medicean manuscript (M); their ascription to one tetralogy is based on their obvious connection with the Danaid myth.

[4] Cf. Tucker's introduction to his edition of the *Suppliants*, p. xxiv; Maurice Croiset, *Eschyle*, p. 48.

[5] *Zagreus*, fr. 5.

Introduction

in relation to that context; in spite of the difficulties of the task, scholarship must attempt to learn all that it can of the meaning of the trilogy to which the *Suppliants* belonged.

A casual reading of the tragedy will reveal the presence of one indisputable theme: the conflict between custom sanctioned by religion (the rights of the suppliant) and political expediency. Other, and perhaps more important, themes have seemed to scholars to be obscured by textual enigmas, by the apparent paucity of explanation of motivation of the action, and by the loss of the second and third members of the trilogy. It is traditionally held that the following basic questions must be answered before the meaning of the *Suppliants* can be discerned: Why did the Danaids flee Egypt and shun marriage with their cousins? Did they possess a legal right to do so? What information can reconstruction of the trilogy supply to clarify the issues and motifs of the extant play?

The first two questions must be regarded as closely interrelated: why do the Danaids flee from the advances of their cousins, and is their refusal of marriage justified in the light of religion, custom, and law? No substantial agreement has been reached in answer to these questions. One school of opinion, marshalled by Wilamowitz, has held that the Danaids refuse marriage because of a thorough misanthropy—*angeborene männerfeindschaft*—which is their principal trait of character.[6] Support for the theory is found in numer-

[6] Wilamowitz's translation of Bamberger's emendation (line 8). See Appendix B.

Introduction

ous statements made by the girls themselves. Perhaps the least ambiguous of these statements is their appeal,

> Ah, may the mighty seed of our holy mother escape the beds of men, unwed, unvanquished. (141-3)

yet such words can be interpreted merely as a logical extension of their abhorrence of the Egyptians, and not as an indication of general misanthropy. No more compelling is the comparison of the Danaids to Amazons (287-9), since in other passages they appear most dependent and feminine.[7]

The majority of critics contend that the Danaids are not misanthropic, but, for varying reasons, are averse only to marriage with the Egyptians. Some claim that it is the brutality and wantonness of their suitors that frightens the maidens;[8] others maintain that the Danaids are asserting their right to refuse enforced marriage.[9] Still others find, on the basis of somewhat dubious evidence, that their refusal is dictated by the belief that marriage within the clan is incestuous and unholy.[10]

[7] Cf. H. W. Smyth, *Aeschylean Tragedy*, p. 57; A. Elisei, "Le Danaidi nelle Supplici di Eschilo," *Studi Italiani di Filologia Classica* 6 (1928), pp. 197ff.

[8] Smyth, *op. cit.*, p. 58; J. Coman, *l'dée de la Némesis chez Eschyle* (Paris, 1931), p. 106.

[9] Cf. Paul Richter, *Zur Dramaturgie des Aeschylus*, pp. 108-9.

[10] Ridgeway, *op. cit.*, pp. 190-5. Cf. Thomson, *op. cit.*, pp. 300-5. This theory rests in part on the fact that the Danaids term marriage with the Egyptians "unholy" (*asebês*, line 9; cf. 223-31). But cf. Vürtheim, *op. cit.*, p. 22, who argues that

Introduction

This latter hypothesis necessitates consideration of the second question, that of the legal status of the Danaids. Thomson, following Ridgeway, argues that the sisters are, by Attic law, in the position of heiresses, and that, when Danaus dies, the Egyptians will even have full claim to them; accordingly, a fifth-century audience would believe that the Danaids were plainly seeking to escape their obligations.[11] Thus the theme of the trilogy is the conflict between two social systems, exogamy and endogamy, with Aeschylus advocating endogamy, the prevailing system of his day.[12]

Ingenious as Thomson's theory is, it has found little support.[13] The Danaids are *not yet* heiresses,[14] and Danaus has by Attic law the right to bestow his daughters in marriage to husbands of his choice, not neces-

---

the impious element in such a union is the violence and compulsion shown by the Egyptians.

[11] *Op. cit.*, pp. 300-5.
[12] *Ibid.*
[13] With the notable exception of Gilbert Norwood, who approves Thomson's interpretation of the *Suppliants* (review of Thomson's *Aeschylus and Athens* in *Classical Philology* 37 [1942], p. 441). For a much less favorable review of Thomson's approach, see A. W. Pickard-Cambridge, *Classical Review* 56 (1942), pp. 21ff. Even the review by A. M. G. Little, *Classical Weekly* 37 (1943), pp. 95-6, who thoroughly admires Thomson's approach, notes that "Thomson's book is an excellent example both of the value and of the dangers of the method."
[14] Ernst Howald, *Die Griechische Tragödie* (Munich, 1930), p. 50. Cf. Bogner, *op. cit.*, p. 106; Philip W. Harsh, *A Handbook of Classical Drama* (Stanford, 1944), p. 446, note 13; Smyth, *op. cit.*, p. 57; Wilamowitz, *op. cit.*, p. 15; Grace Macurdy, "Had The Danaid Trilogy a Social Problem?" *Classical Philology* 39 (1944), pp. 95-100.

Introduction

sarily to the next of kin.[15] Accordingly, the flight of the maidens is both morally and legally justified.[16]

Such total disagreement impels one to wonder whether many scholars have not been on the wrong scent, and whether Aeschylus did not intend to take any definite stand on this moral and legal issue. May it not be that the vexing obscurity of the text at crucial points is intentional, and not just a result of textual corruption?[17] Coman, for one, believes this to be so, and holds that the problem will probably remain insoluble precisely because Aeschylus had no intention of dealing here with questions of law.[18] Perhaps the issue of the Danaids' legal and moral position at the beginning of the *Suppliants* has been a chimaera, diverting scholarship from the real dramatic cruces.

Reconstructions of the trilogy have abounded for more than a century. Unfortunately, many of the theories are as fanciful as the evidence is sparse. There is little overt foreshadowing in the extant play (although

---

[15] Cf. Macurdy, *op. cit.* She cites as evidence Isaeus 10.13 and 9.29.

[16] Little support has been given Wilamowitz, who asserts that the Egyptians regard themselves as the Danaids' masters because they have won them by right of conquest, in a battle fought prior to the action of the play. He relies on the slim internal evidence of lines 84-5 and 741-2 (*op. cit.*, p. 15). For a refutation of his argument, see Friedrich Focke, "Aeschylos Hiketiden," *Nachrichten von der Königlichen Gesellschaft der Wissenschaften zu Göttingen* (1922), pp. 172-3.

[17] Walter Headlam, *Classical Review* 14 (1900), pp. 111-2, writes: "It can hardly be that this obscurity is other than designed . . . perhaps it was a question Aeschylus did not care to argue."

[18] *Op. cit.*, p. 105.

Introduction

much inheres in the imagery, as I hope to show later), and the fragments of the lost plays are disappointingly uninformative, since they must be located in a hypothetical reconstruction before they can take on meaning. Confronted with this poverty of information, scholars have turned for assistance to the many ancient treatments of the Danaid myth,[19] a hazardous practice, since the critic's decision as to which version is the Aeschylean must rest, in the last analysis, on *a priori* judgment. The broader outline of the plots of the lost plays can safely be assumed, however, to be that given by Aeschylus in the *Prometheus Bound*, where it is related that forty-nine of the maidens slew their husbands, while the fiftieth, Hypermnestra, spared hers, and founded with him a royal line. All other detail, both prior to and subsequent to the murder, cannot with reason be reconstructed by appeal to the authority of non-Aeschylean myth.

The problem of reconstruction justly centers on the interpretation of the only really significant fragment, the speech of Aphrodite from the *Danaids*; information regarding the *Egyptians* is so scanty that all one may

[19] The myth, which appears in prose and poetry from Hesiod to the late poets and mythographers, is reported with so many variations that any full recapitulation of it lies beyond the range of this essay. For sources and bibliography, see Campbell Bonner, "A Study of the Danaid Myth," *Harvard Studies in Classical Philology* 13 (1902), pp. 129-73; Vürtheim, *op. cit.*, pp. 1-29 and *passim*; Wasser's article in *Real-Encyclopädie* 4², cols. 2087-91, *s.v.* "Danaïdes"; Bethe, *ibid.*, cols. 2091-2, *s.v.* Danaïs; G. A. Megas, "Die Sage von Danaos und den Danaiden," *Hermes* 68 (1933), pp. 415-28; A. Nathansky, "Des Aischylos Danais," *Wiener Studien* 32 (1910), pp. 9-12.

Introduction

properly assume is that the marriage of the cousins, or preparations for it, took place in the play. Some believe that the title indicates that the Egyptians formed the chorus,[20] but even this is open to dispute.[21] Possibly, as the majority of critics hold, the results of an offstage battle, in which Pelasgus was killed (to be replaced as king by Danaus) and the Egyptians were victorious, compelled the Danaids to submit to marriage;[22] it might be a good guess that the murder occurred in the interval between the second and third plays.[23] One cannot, however, entertain these hypotheses with confidence.

The situation is somewhat different with the final play, the *Danaids*, since the speech of Aphrodite (fragment 44) affords tangible, if slight, evidence for reconstruction. This fragment has been most commonly linked to one of two alternative traditions: the story told by Pausanias (2.19.6) that Hypermnestra was brought to trial on a charge of disobedience and acquitted; the tradition found in Euripides (*Orestes*

---

[20] Cf. Bogner, *op. cit.*, p. 121; Carl Steinweg, *Aischylos*, p. 14; von Fritz, *op. cit.*, p. 127.

[21] Cf. Croiset, *op. cit.*, p. 69.

[22] Cf. Bogner, *op. cit.*, p. 121; Franz Stoessl, *Die Trilogie des Aischylos*, p. 104. Wilamowitz (*op. cit.*, p. 20) suggests that Pelasgus effected a compromise by which the Danaids were recognized as citizens and married their cousins with the proviso that the latter were not to become their *kektêmenoi* (see line 337). The flaw in this theory has been exposed by von Fritz (*op. cit.*, p. 128), who observes that such a solution makes the motive for the murder difficult to explain.

[23] Cf. von Fritz, *op. cit.*, p. 129; F. G. Welcker, "Aegypter und Danaiden," *Rheinisches Museum für Philologie* 4 (1846), p. 498.

Introduction

871-3 and *schol. ad loc.*) that Aegyptus, father of the slain brothers, prosecuted Danaus, and presumably his daughters as well, for murder. Those who believe that Aeschylus followed the first of these traditions maintain that fragment 44 is an excerpt from a speech made by Aphrodite in defense of the maiden who spared her husband;[24] their conclusion is based in part on analogy with the court scene of the *Eumenides*.[25] This theory, which I find attractive, has recently been attacked by von Fritz, but I feel that his principal criticism is largely subjective. He believes that the three plays would be far less unified if the concluding drama were focused on Hypermnestra, rather than on the fate of the Danaids.[26] I shall attempt to show later that the story of Hypermnestra was a unifying rather than a distracting force in the plot of the trilogy, and that the murderous deed of the other Danaids was not made light of[27] if the story of their expiation was not the central theme of the final play.

Few scholars have withstood the temptation to reconstruct the *Danaids* by analogy with the *Eumenides* and the trial of Orestes. Croiset, however, contends that the availability of only two actors at the time of

[24] Cf. Bogner, *op. cit.*, pp. 122-3; Sheppard, *op. cit.*, p. 221; Smyth, *op. cit.*, p. 44; Thomson, *op. cit.*, p. 306; Tucker, *op. cit.*, p. xxv; Vürtheim, *op. cit.*, pp. 71-6.

[25] Others, notably Robertson, *op. cit.*, have expressed the view that the words of Aphrodite could have served as well for a prosecution speech arraigning Danaus and the guilty sisters. But see von Fritz, *op. cit.*, pp. 249-50, for a criticism of this view.

[26] *Op. cit.*, p. 251.
[27] *Ibid.*

Introduction

the production militates against the likelihood of a court scene; he concludes that Hypermnestra was condemned by her father and saved by the intervention of Aphrodite.[28] This possibility cannot be lightly regarded.

If the Danaids were not brought to trial, they must still have been punished in some manner for their blood guilt, since it is not easy to believe that Aeschylus fully condoned their deed. Vürtheim, however, has shown rather conclusively that the legend of the Danaids' underworld labors is post-Aeschylean,[29] and the mass slaying of a tragic chorus seems singularly unGreek. The most popular conjecture has been that Aeschylus followed the tradition found in the scholiast to Pindar (*Pythian* 9.112) and in Pausanias (3.12.1-2) that Danaus betrothed his daughters to the victors in a foot race, perhaps at the command of Aphrodite.[30]

D. S. Robertson's treatment of the problem is of

[28] *Op. cit.*, p. 70. Cf. Marie Delcourt, *Eschyle*, p. 45. Wilamowitz believes a trial unlikely because Aeschylus was not yet capable of creating a trial scene like that of the *Eumenides* (*op. cit.*, p. 23). Von Fritz (*op. cit.*, pp. 265-8) thinks it likely that the concluding tragedy contained the atonement of the Danaids and their betrothal to another group of suitors; the speech of Aphrodite was then delivered in connection with the preparations for this second marriage. I shall not pause to summarize the fullest attempt at reconstruction, that of Stoessl (*op. cit.*). The result of his effort, ingenious as it is, is primarily of interest only as an example of the scholarly futility of unchecked fancy and *a priori* methods.

[29] *Op. cit.*, pp. 25-6.

[30] Cf. Bogner, *op. cit.*, p. 124; Croiset, *op. cit.*, pp. 70-1; Wilamowitz, *op. cit.*, p. 23. See below, p. 86.

Introduction

some interest.[31] True, he commits the same error as does von Fritz, in assuming that the question of the Danaids' guilt must have been the central theme of the last play, and that, therefore, the story of the maidens, instead of that of Hypermnestra, must have formed the center of interest; he fails to recognize that the solution of the question is implicit in the story of the acquittal of the maiden who spared her husband, and that the forced marriage of the Danaids to other suitors would emphasize their guilt. On the other hand, his suggestion that the *Danaids* concluded with the founding of the Thesmophoria[32] as an institution safeguarding woman's dignity[33] is a provocative contribution. Unfortunately, the connection of the festival with the trilogy cannot be established with any certainty,[34] and must be recognized only as a possibility.

In summary, no substantial agreement has been reached in interpretation of the play; much, therefore, remains to be done. But what new light can be brought to bear on a literary problem that has for many decades attracted the close scrutiny of capable scholars? Of the critical methods employed, only that of social criticism

---

[31] *Op. cit.*

[32] Herodotus (2.171) asserts that the Danaids brought to Greece a mystical cult of Demeter, which later became the Thesmophoria.

[33] *Op. cit.*, p. 53. Thomson, *op. cit.*, p. 308, accepts this theory with a few modifications.

[34] Vürtheim, in fact, criticizes the theory on the ground that there is no evidence in the ritual of this festival that Demeter *Thesmophoros* was regarded as a protectress of woman's marriage rights (*op. cit.*, pp. 74-5).

Introduction

has not been fully explored,[35] yet it is doubtful that even it can furnish the needed insights without the aid of additional information from another source. The answer lies, I believe, in a return to careful examination of the text of the *Suppliants*, and, in particular, the imagery of the play; the latter is a source of information which, with sporadic exceptions, has been overlooked by otherwise methodical and alert critics. Too frequently the imagery of Greek drama has been regarded as pleasant but basically meaningless and frivolous ornament not organically integrated with the "thought" of poetry. It is my objective to show, within the limited scope of a discussion of one play, that the imagery of an Aeschylean tragedy can be a vitally important vehicle of meaning; that the *Suppliants*, in particular, cannot be fully understood without the careful study of this aspect of the dramatic creation.[36]

Specifically, it is my intention to demonstrate that the web of imagery woven around Io, the ancestress of the Danaids, conveys much of the meaning of the *Suppliants*, that the story of Io is intended as an "allegory" explaining with remarkable clarity and completeness the character and motives of the Danaids, and is thereby the ultimate vehicle of the basic ideas ex-

[35] I have not dealt with the Procrustean approach of George Thomson (*op. cit.*), who forgets, in the heat of his doctrinaire fervor, that Aeschylus was primarily concerned with religious and moral problems, and not with the patterns of the dialectic.

[36] Robert F. Goheen's *The Imagery of Sophocles' Antigone* (Princeton, 1951) provides a good example of the value of such study.

Introduction

pressed in the trilogy.[37] The significance of this imagery has been suggested by several scholars, but no one has as yet undertaken to investigate it, in all its ramifications, thoroughly and systematically. J. T. Sheppard, in a brilliant but brief article published early in the century,[38] called attention to the importance of the Io imagery and discussed a few of its implications, but did not examine the problem in any detail or pursue its logical implications; unfortunately, other scholars appear to be unfamiliar with or unconvinced by his work. A few other critics, it is true, have observed that the relationship of Io and the Danaids holds some dramatic significance, but have not gone far beyond the simple observation.[39] Only O. Hiltbrunner, in an excellent recent study, has shown clearly the importance of the Io theme, but he has not, I feel, sufficiently developed the significance of the motif in terms of the trilogy.[40] More commonly, the imagery

---

[37] Allegory, as used here of extended metaphor operative within the tragedy in the manner described, might be termed "secondary," whereas if the story of the *dramatis personae* (the Danaids) possessed allegorical significance, it could, in contrast, be designated as "primary."

[38] *Op. cit.*

[39] Cf. Georges Méautis, *Eschyle et la Trilogie*, p. 55; Mazon, *op. cit.*, p. 6; C. R. Post, "The Dramatic Art of Aeschylus," *Harvard Studies in Classical Philology* 16 (1905), p. 33. Both Gilbert Murray (*Aeschylus, the Creator of Tragedy*, p. 36) and Thomson (*op. cit.*, p. 300) display a somewhat deeper insight into the Io-Danaid parallel. E. T. Owen, in *The Harmony of Aeschylus*, pp. 5-8, is even more perceptive than Murray and Thomson.

[40] *Wiederholungs- und Motivtechnik bei Aischylos*, pp. 7-41. Hiltbrunner's analysis came to my attention after I had completed my preparations for this study; I was interested to dis-

Introduction

of Io is thought to be a rather tedious poetic decoration; one scholar even observes that the Io motif is not an essential element of the poetic economy and that Aeschylus added the story of Io to the tragedy only because he knew that his audience took pleasure in such stories.[41] A more recent critic, although admitting the existence of some parallel between Io and the Danaids, has said that "this mythological material is developed and expanded on a scale that is out of proportion to its dramatic relevance,"[42] while another has expressed surprise at the fact that Aeschylus refers in detail to the remote ancestry of the Danaids (the Io story) but says so little of the more recent antecedents of the action.[43] It is my hope to prove that the allegory of Io is not only "dramatically relevant" to the Danaid trilogy but altogether indispensable to its correct interpretation.

---

cover that we had arrived independently at rather similar attitudes toward several of the principal images of the play. I shall refer in notes below to specific agreements and divergences in our analyses.

[41] Richter, *op. cit.*, p. 111.

[42] H. G. Robertson, "*Dikê* and *Hybris* in Aeschylus' Suppliants," *Classical Review* 50 (1936), p. 106.

[43] Von Fritz, *op. cit.*, p. 126.

II. The Imagery of the *Suppliants*

THE recurring comparisons of the situation of the Danaids with that of their ancestress Io fall into three categories; (1) direct appeals by the Danaids to Zeus, as the lover and savior of Io or to Epaphus, the product of Zeus' union with Io;[1] (2) direct references to Io and her story; (3) indirect comparisons, suggested by image association or emanating from direct comparisons weighted with overtones of dramatic irony. Each category includes both comparisons significant principally in context and others which foreshadow events to occur in the second and third members of the trilogy (or even beyond the framework of the trilogy). The latter are obviously more vital for reconstruction of subsequent action, but not necessarily more informative for the themes of the drama.

(1) The direct appeals are sufficiently numerous and their application manifest enough to establish beyond question the fact and significance of the comparison of the fifty maidens with Io; Aeschylus did not employ his images loosely or uneconomically, as studies of the *Agamemnon* have shown.[2] Superficially, the ap-

[1] It is to be noted that the Danaids never appeal to Io for protection. The reason is clear: Io is a mortal, and powerless to help. Her role is passive; the agents are Zeus and Epaphus.
[2] Cf. W. B. Stanford, *Greek Metaphor* (Oxford, 1936).

Imagery of the *Suppliants*

peals serve merely to substantiate the Danaids' claim to asylum in Argos through their kinship with Argive Io. If this were the sole *raison d'être* of the appeals, however, there would have been no practical reason for their repetition after the announcement by Danaus that asylum had been granted (lines 600ff.); the final strophe of the play is sufficient evidence that the image had not been discarded upon the expiration of its superficial utility for purposes of plot.[3]

The direct appeals, which occur frequently in the drama, should be examined first. As one might expect, Zeus is most often addressed. At times he is approached in general terms in his varied but more traditional aspects; more frequently, he is invoked as Io's lover and savior, or as ancestor of the Danaids.

The first indisputable appeal to Zeus as lover, savior, and ancestor is that of the chorus in lines 162-75. The first line of the ephymnion clearly indicates that here he is called on because of his connection with Io. In the antistrophe, lines 168-75, the Danaids implicitly assert their descent from Zeus by predicting his ignominy if he dishonors

> the child of the cow . . . the child whom
> he himself, long ago, begot.

Curiously enough, the Danaids are so profoundly affected by the awareness of the story of their progeni-

[3] Sheppard, *op. cit.*, pp. 222ff., and Hiltbrunner, *op. cit.*, pp. 7-41, both call attention to the relationship between the vicissitudes of Io and those of the Danaids.

Imagery of the *Suppliants*

tors that they here virtually identify themselves with Epaphus, the immediate offspring of Zeus and Io.

The majestic deity portrayed in the choral ode 524-99 is explicitly identified as *ephaptor* ("toucher" or "caresser")—both lover and savior—of Io (535), father of Epaphus (580-1), and ancestor of the Danaids (588-9). The entire ode is permeated with the conception of Zeus as personally implicated in the fortunes of the fifty sisters.

The important closing lines of the tragedy prove that the emphasis on the bond between Zeus and Io is not accidental. Zeus is summoned to preserve the Danaids from marriage with their cousins,

> that very god who delivered Io from torment
> (1064-5).

In other instances Zeus is invoked in a manner which appears to indicate a constant consciousness in the suppliants' minds of his alliance with Io and relation to her descendants. The "gods of the race" of line 77 and "father" of line 811 are to be considered in their particular as well as general applications.

The Danaids do, of course, pray to Zeus in his more traditional aspects as well; as suppliants, they call on Zeus *hikesios* (347) or *hiktaios* (385), and threaten to turn to "the Zeus of the dead" (158). One is, however, justified in assuming that the audience, so thoroughly prepared by the consistency of the poet's expression, should have been at all times conscious of the peculiar relationship involving Zeus, Io, and the Danaids. Having conditioned his audience, Aeschylus

Imagery of the *Suppliants*

was enabled to weave the tapestry of his imagery with great subtlety.

Epaphus, son of Zeus and Io, forefather of the Danaids, and savior in his own right, is the recipient of at least one appeal. His aid is entreated in 40-56, where he is addressed as "divine calf." Probably he is to be included with Zeus among the "gods of the race" of line 77.

(2) Direct reference to the Io story is made frequently by the Danaids. Such references occur throughout the drama, ranging from seemingly casual allusions to fully developed descriptions. The most complete example of the latter is found in the dialogue between Pelasgus and the chorus, lines 291-319; these lines serve the immediate function of establishing kinship rights between the Danaids and Argos. Many of these allusions can be explained, however, only as part of the poetic tissue, and not as an element of skeletal plot structure. A brief analysis of the patent references to Io should reveal how vital this imagery is to the interpretation of the play.

The initial reference to the story of Io may possibly occur in line 8.[4] Lines 16-18,

> Our race that boasts its birth from the gadfly-driven heifer at the touch and on-breathing of Zeus

explicitly identify the Danaids as descendants of Io and Zeus. The occurrence of these references so early in the parodos is clear indication that the Danaid-Io

[4] See Appendix B.

Imagery of the *Suppliants*

relationship is important to the content. The triad of Zeus, Io, and Epaphus is invoked in lines 40-47. Lines 162-7 refer to Io's flight; 168-75 to the kinship of the chorus with Zeus. 206 alludes briefly to the kinship. In 275, the chorus first informs Pelasgus of its descent from Io. 291-319 develop the claim fully and rehearse the tale of Io and Zeus both for the sake of plot, and to point up subsequent imagery. The choral passage 524-99 is centered on the Io-Zeus-Danaid relationship.[5] Direct references to the Io tale are then lacking, from 599 until the final strophe of the play, 1062-7, where Zeus as Io's lover is addressed. This lack can be explained by the fact that the physical action of the drama occurs between these two points; the reflective portions of the play offer greater opportunity for development of significant imagery.

So much for the direct appeals to Zeus as Io's lover and savior, and for the direct allusions to the story of Io; their presence could be dismissed as contributing merely to the line of the plot, even though their extreme frequency should render suspect such a conclusion. All doubt of the significance of the Io allegory for the interpretation of the drama is dispelled, however, when one examines the complex tissue of imagery which the poet develops from the comparison of Io and the Danaids.

(3) There are, in the *Suppliants*, four major or key images. Each emanates naturally and consistently from the Zeus-Io legend; they are interwoven with subtle intricacy, recurring with variations in mood and sig-

[5] See above, p. 20.

Imagery of the *Suppliants*

nificance as the drama evolves. Some appear less frequently than others, but it is dangerous to conclude that they are, therefore, "less important"; it is the total web of imagery which is important and meaningful, not the sum of its parts.

These four images may be designated for convenience, roughly in the order of frequency of occurrence, as (1) bull and cow; (2) contrast of male and female; (3) touch and seizure; (4) breath, wind, and storm.[6] A separate examination of each image will be of value in demonstrating how the figures develop and shift with the evolution of the play. Their larger significance will be discussed below, in Chapter IV.

The imagery of bull and cow. The symbol or image of the bull and cow (*bous*) derives obviously from the play's basic allegory, the story of Zeus and Io. Frequency of reference to this legend establishes it in the mind of the audience or reader as vital to the poet's meaning; each further allusion to bull or cow redirects the attention of the audience to the fundamental significance of the allegory.

Mention of the cow occurs first in line 17, clustered with the images of touch and breath; thus three of the four key images occur conjointly on their first appearance. Here, of course, the reference is explanatory and preparatory.

[6] Hiltbrunner, *op. cit.*, stresses (3) and (4) as motifs, but also sees such terms as marriage (*gamos*) and *polis* as *motivwörter*. If they are, they must be very weak ones, since the context of plot demands frequent appearance of such common words.

Imagery of the *Suppliants*

In lines 40-47, the chorus calls on the "divine calf" Epaphus, the son of the *progonou boös* ("the cow, our ancestress"); again breath (*epipnoia*) and touch (*ephapsis*) occur in conjunction with the reference to bull and cow as an element of preparatory narrative. The image is developed further in the antistrophe (49-56), as the chorus announces that it has come to the "grazing places" of its ancestress; we begin to observe that the chorus identifies its own story, in some degree, with that of Io.

Bull and cow are suggested in 118 and the suggestion is repeated in 129 as the chorus invokes the *Apian bounin* ("hilly Apian land"). Probably there is amphiboly in these words: *Apian* denotes Apis, the medicine-priest "from beyond Naupactus" (262-3), but surely suggests Apis, the Egyptian bull god and counterpart of Epaphus; the validity of this conclusion is confirmed by the proximity of the rare word *bounin* with its suggestion of *bous*.[7]

Bous is used again in 170 as descriptive of Io, mother of Epaphus; Zeus is warned against treating with dishonor the "child of the cow." Literally, of course, the child of the cow is Epaphus; however, the chorus appears to be intensifying its sense of identification with the ancestral line, since any dishonor to Epaphus is in this case figurative, and the phrase is only a circumlocution for dishonor to the Danaids themselves. Increasingly they think of themselves as "children of the cow."

[7] Sheppard (*op. cit.*, p. 226), Hiltbrunner (*op. cit.*, pp. 14-15), and Owen (*op. cit.*, p. 10) all realize the connotations of these words.

Imagery of the *Suppliants*

In line 275, the chorus announces itself to Pelasgus as the "seed of the fruitful cow"—the Danaids' sense of oneness with their progenitors is again marked. The curious tale of Apis, the medicine-priest, precedes these words (lines 260-70); as observed above, this name appears ambiguous and surely carries the connotation of the bull deity.[8] Epaphus, moreover, like the Northern Greek Apis described in this passage, was known for his remarkable therapeutic abilities. No further connection between the two can be determined, but the similarity of name and function is too striking to be thought coincidental.

The chorus proceeds to reinforce its demand for asylum by drawing from the king's memory the tale of Io (291-324). We should expect the recurrence of words for bull and cow in this narrative passage as a matter of course, since the metamorphoses of Zeus and Io are an essential element of the legend. We find, however, that in the twenty-four lines from 291 to 315, *bous* or one of its compounds occurs eight times, *tauros* ("bull") and *portis* ("calf") once each: 299, *boun*; 300, *boï*; 301, *bouthorô* and *taurô*; 303, *boï*; 304, *oioboukolon*; 306, *boï*; 307, *boêlatên*; 314, *portis* and *boös*. Surely the impact of this staccato repetition is effective in re-emphasizing to the audience the importance of the bull-cow imagery, and consequently the significance of the Io allegory.

The choral exchange between the Danaids and Pelasgus (348-417), which follows their trimeter dialogue, opens pregnantly with a metaphor in which

[8] See the second paragraph preceding.

Imagery of the *Suppliants*

the fifty maidens compare themselves to a frightened heifer:

> Behold me your suppliant, the far-coursed [*peridromon*] fugitive [*phygada*], like a wolf-pursued heifer among the sheer crags, where confident of rescue she lows to tell the herdsman of her distress. (350-3)

Obviously the chorus, subconsciously at least, identifies itself with the Io heifer. *Phygada* and *peridromon* are descriptive both of Io and the Danaids; Pelasgus is, of course, the herdsman who alone can aid the fifty maidens. They are in an untenable position without his protection, as was the harassed fugitive Io without the protection of the "herdsman" Zeus. The thoughts of the Danaids dwell ever more on the similarity between Io's situation and their own.

Bouchilon, an unusual compound of *bous*, occurs in 540, in a passage descriptive of Io, and is soon followed by *boukolou* in 557. The description of Io's flight proceeds to her depiction in 568-70 as "a being fused of beast and mortal, part cow, part woman." The Danaids, too, are part woman and in part the reincarnation of their cow ancestress. Words deriving from the same root as *bous* or resembling it in sound are found in abundance throughout the latter portion of this choral song dealing with Io and Zeus: *boukolou* (557), *pamboton* (558), *chionoboskon* (559), *boton* (568), *boös* (569), *ethamboun* (570), *labousa* (580), *boa* (583), *epiboulous* (587) and *boulios* (599). The repetition of this explosive, dominant

Imagery of the *Suppliants*

sound, resembling the sound of the key word in one of the key images of the drama, is surely the product of the poet's conscious craftsmanship.

Pelasgus, in line 620, terms the pollution which will arise from the refusal of asylum to the Danaids an insurmountable *boskêma* (literally "herd of cattle") of woe. The Danaids, in the choral song that follows, pray that the cattle of Argos shall be fertile (*bot'* ... *polygona telethoi*) (691-2), and that the inhabitants shall worship the gods with *bouthoutoisi timais* ("honors of slain oxen") (706). In 776, the *ga bouni*, "land of the cow" as well as "land of hills," is again invoked by the chorus; the invocation is followed by a reference to the Apian land (*Apias chthonos*), suggestive once more of Apis and Epaphus (777-8). The waters of the Nile are described as *alphesiboion* ("yielding fat cattle"—i.e., Io, Epaphus?) in 855. Pelasgus uses *aboukolêton* ("untended," as of oxen) of the thought suggested by the herald (929). At this point, the bull-cow imagery ceases, and greater use is made of other imagery, including, however, metaphorical comparison of the Io cow and the Danaids (cf. 1017 and 1064-7). In summary, this image, while more direct and somewhat less subtle than the other key images, is recurrent and indisputably effective in focusing the attention of the audience on the central extended metaphor of the *Suppliants*.

The imagery of contrast of male and female. The Danaids emphasize throughout the play their femininity and contrast to it the predatory masculinity of the

Imagery of the *Suppliants*

generic male, particularly as exemplified in the Egyptians. The image derives logically from the antithesis inherent in the legend of the Zeus bull and the Io cow, and serves to cast further light on the nearly pathological workings of the minds of the maidens. Like the bull and cow image, to which it is closely related, it is less complex than the remaining key images; the latter form, in a sense, a superstructure of metaphor built on the foundation of these two simpler images.

The male-female contrast is perhaps hinted at first by the chorus in line 8, when it describes marriage with the Egyptians as "self-produced" by the males.[9] Later in the parodos, the contrast is made explicit; the Danaids are a *hiketês thêlugenês stolos* ("suppliant band of women"), while the Egyptians are characterized as an *arsenoplêthês d' hesmos hybristês* ("thronging swarm of violent men") (27-30). This contrast, which suggests that the female is weak and pious,[10] while the male is powerful and wicked, forms a theme which is reproduced with variations through the remainder of the play, always with the story of Io looming meaningfully behind it.

The weakness of the female is emphasized in the words of the chorus,

> I wound my tender cheek burnt by the Nile
> and my heart that has known no tears.
> (70-2)

[9] See Appendix B.
[10] *Stolos* ("band") is often used of a military expedition (cf. *Agamemnon* 45). Its appearance here may convey an ironic and prophetic suggestion of the violence now latent in the maidens, but to emerge murderously later in the trilogy.

Imagery of the *Suppliants*

and again later, as the Danaids implore their father not to leave them:

> Leave me not alone, I beg you, father. A woman left alone is nothing—the Spirit of War lives not in her. (748-9)

The gods are requested not to allow the young men to get the upper hand in, we must infer, the struggle with the female (79-80). The chorus prays that it will escape the beds of men (141-3 and repeated in 151-3). Sexual symbolism appears to be present in the prayer to Artemis, whom the chorus describes as "holding in safety the holy walls" (146), and who, as virgin goddess (*admêta*, 149) is invoked to aid the virgin Danaids. Such symbolic use of the building or its parts is paralleled by *Seven Against Thebes*, 454-6:

> before he bursts into my abode and despoils,
> with arrogant spear, my maiden's bower.

and *Choephoroe*, 71-2;

> But for him who attempts the bridal bower
> there is no cure

Chastity is, in these lines, considered as characteristic of the female, as opposed to the violent lust (*hybrin broteion*, 104-5) of the male. Pelasgus, not entirely unobservant, perceives this obsession of the Danaids, when he compares them to *anandrous . . . Amazonas* ("mateless Amazons," 287).

The male-female contrast is heavily underlined again in the choral prayer of thanks to Argos:

Imagery of the *Suppliants*

> Nor did they cast their votes for the males,
> despising the women's cause (643-5)

and in the threat of the Egyptian herald and Pelasgus' answer to it:

> [Herald] May victory and mastery rest with the men!
> [King] Nay, men, you will find, are the dwellers in this land. (951-3)

In many other instances, the contrast is strongly implied, if not explicitly made:

> Chorus. Never may I fall into the hands and mastery of (these?) men. (392-3)

> Chorus. But recognize the violent lust [*hybrin*] of (these?) men (426)

> [King] And perhaps some, in pity at the sight, will hate the lust [*hybrin*] of this company of men (486-7)

> Chorus. ward off the lust [*hybrin*] of men (528)

> Chorus. For the male race of Aegyptus, intolerable in its lust [*hybrin*] (817-8)

> Chorus. And may he award victory to the women! (1068-9)

Imagery of the *Suppliants*

It is perhaps significant that in four of the six passages cited here, violent lust—*hybris*—is immediately associated with the male. Similar association is made in two of the examples given earlier.[11] *Hybris*, then, is without question the dominant characteristic of the male, in the eyes of the Danaids.

Lines 659-60 contain a strikingly ambiguous metaphor:

> μήποτε λοιμὸς ἀνδρῶν
> τάνδε πόλιν κενῶσαι·

Translators, who usually and properly render them as "Let pestilence never empty this city of men," have understood correctly the denotation; we may, however, translate "Let pestilence of men never devastate this city," thus investing the words *loimos* and *andrôn* with significant ambiguity (cf. 951-3, cited above).

As in the case of the other key images, the male-female contrast is dependent on the fundamental allegory of the drama, the Io story, and develops with poetic logic from that legend. The chorus of Danaids reminds us of this when it prays to Zeus,

> Looking on our race of *women*, old in story,
> recall the joyous tale of the beloved *woman*
> who was our ancestress. (531-4)

Zeus is invoked to protect the women who are the palingenesis of his beloved Io, in blood and consciousness of sex.

[11] p. 29.

Imagery of the *Suppliants*

The imagery of touch and seizure. The image of touch and seizure is more sophisticated and complex than the two key images discussed above; like them, it derives from the legend of Io, but from one of its more poetic, even mystical, aspects. It is correspondingly less obvious. The intent of the dramatist can, none the less, be discovered if the figure is carefully analyzed.

"Touch" in the sense intended here means "gentle touch" or "caress." "Seizure" should be understood to signify violent laying on of hands, and to connote violence and predatory force in general. Aeschylus skillfully develops the tension in this image, as he varies it from pole to counterpole, and again to an ambiguous neutrality.[12]

The image of touch and seizure has, as its point of departure, the legend of the conception of Epaphus and the similarity of his name to and possibly correct derivation from the word ἀφή, meaning "touch" or "caress." If this derivation is historically incorrect, it may well have been originated by Aeschylus, since no allusion is made to it by his predecessors, or by his contemporary, Pindar.

The path is opened for development of this image, as for the two images previously discussed, by preparation made in the parodos:

> Our race that boasts its birth from the gadfly-driven heifer at the touch [*epaphês*] and on-breathing [*epipnoias*] of Zeus (16-18).

[12] Sheppard, elsewhere so perceptive, sees in this image only the motif of healing by laying on of hands (*op. cit.*, p. 225). Hiltbrunner (*op. cit.*, p. 34) properly emphasizes the ambiguity of the image.

Imagery of the *Suppliants*

Development is soon continued, as the chorus tells the story of the conception and birth of Epaphus:

> and the fated time brought his [Zeus's] touch [*ephapsin*] to fulfillment in accordance with the word, and she gave birth to Epaphus. (45-7)

The poet thus informs us that the name Epaphus derives from the manner of his begetting, and that we are to be conscious of this fact when his name is mentioned. The denotation of *ephapsis* is here "caress" or "gentle touch," a touch that delivers from pain; the word is still univalent at this stage in the evolution of the image.

Lines 313-15 introduce a new and vital word into the image:

> Chorus. And Zeus, her caresser [*ephaptôr*], implanted the seed with his hand.
> King. Who then claims to be the cow's divine calf?
> Chorus. Epaphus, named truly for ῥυσίων.

One may paraphrase freely as "Zeus the caresser implanted with his hand the seed of Epaphus, named rightly for *hrusion*." Why the introduction of a new word *hrusion*, when we are quite aware that the presumed derivation of Epaphus is from *haphê* or *epaphan*? Has the new word been introduced for the sake of metre or variety? Unequivocally no. *Hrusion* is by no means a synonym of *haphê*; its meaning is so en-

33

Imagery of the *Suppliants*

tirely different that the reader is startled when he meets it where he is anticipating a form of *ephapsis* or *epaphê*. Aeschylus has vitalized his image with a violent and sudden twist which should prepare the audience for significant variation in later lines.

Indeed, many translators have evidently been unable to resist the strength of their anticipation, and have rendered line 315 as "Epaphus, so named with truth from the laying on of hands."[13] Others, including Mazon,[14] Hiltbrunner,[15] and Vürtheim,[16] have seen that *hrusion* is not simply equivalent to *ephapsis*; Mazon, for example, translates as "Épaphos, dont le nom véridique dit la délivrance d'Io." What actually does *hrusion* mean? Fundamentally, "surety" or "pledge"; it may also mean "reprisal" or "deliverance," and finally, "stolen property taken back as compensation" (cf. *Agamemnon*, 535); it is a word which often connotes violence. Vürtheim is probably correct in suggesting that Aeschylus here derives the name Epaphus *ek tou ephaptesthai tôn hrusiôn* ("from laying hands on the surety") and by ellipsis abbreviates the derivation to *ek tôn hrusiôn* ("from the surety").[17] He can cite in support of his interpretation the lines of Sophocles (*Oedipus at Colonus*, 858-9), where *hrusion* and *ephaptomai* occur in conjunction:

[13] Tucker's translation. So also H. W. Smyth.
[14] See his edition.
[15] *Op. cit.*, p. 28.
[16] *Op. cit.*, commentary for line 312.
[17] "Hier schiebt sich im Geiste des Dichters das Bild der Pfändung vor dasjenige der Zeugung mit der Hand und er lässt den Epaphos gennant werden *ek tou ephaptesthai* (*tôn hrusiôn*). Kurzer noch *ek tôn hrusiôn!*" (*ibid.*)

Imagery of the *Suppliants*

Then a greater surety [*hrusion*] you shall
soon give to the city, for I will lay hands
[*ephapsomai*] on more than these two girls.

This interpretation seems to be more acceptable than that of Mazon, which appears to make little sense. Aeschylus, then, has omitted only the word *ephapsis* and not the concept; he has, on the other hand, added a new concept to the image. The seizure of Io by Zeus takes on an implication of violence, and the image, previously simple, has now acquired fresh and suggestive overtones.[18]

The audience is then fully prepared for the words of Pelasgus (412), which shift the metaphor from recollection to anticipation; "that strife may not seize on you for prize" (*hrusiôn ephapsetai*). Here the image is clearly one of violent seizure. Although the words apply to the Danaids, the audience necessarily is reminded of Io and her seizure and caress at the hands of Zeus. The thread of imagery binds the Danaids and Io still closer.

The verbal form of *hrusion* appears a few lines later, as the Danaids call on Pelasgus for protection; "and see me not seized [*hrusiastheisan*] from this sanctuary of many gods" (423-4). Their plea is that they may be spared the violent seizure experienced by Io. The parallel in these lines between ancestress and descendants is strengthened by the fact that Io had been a priestess of Hera, and her wanderings had begun from

---

[18] It is interesting to note that *hrusion* occurs five times in the *Suppliants* and only once elsewhere in Aeschylean tragedy (*Agamemnon*, 535).

Imagery of the *Suppliants*

the shrine of a goddess (cf. 291-2). The lines of the chorus immediately preceding, "the fugitive . . . driven from afar by godless banishment" (420-2) are eminently descriptive of Io as well as the Danaids.

Amphiboly in line 535 varies the image in color. The chorus prays to Zeus, γενοῦ πολυμνήστωρ, ἔφαπτορ Ἰοῦς. *Polymnêstôr* ambiguously signifies both "rememberer" and, by analogy of sound, πολυμνηστήρ, "frequently a husband (or suitor)."[19] The effect of this connotation is to emphasize the sexual aspect of *ephaptôr*.

The touch of Zeus is further characterized as "might and harmless strength"—βίᾳ δ' ἀπηματοσθενεῖ[20]—in line 576. Here the conflict of opposites, gentle touch and violent seizure, appears reconciled in the mystery of the divine. Zeus' intercourse with Io is at once violent and gentle; she is taken by force, yet her misfortunes cease as a product of that force.

The image is again focused directly on the Danaids, when Danaus tells his daughters,

> perhaps some herald or envoys may come
> eager to abduct you, seizing on you for prize
> [*hrusiôn ephaptores*] (727-8).

They are threatened, as was their ancestress, by a male violence.

Yet that violence appears in a different, although

---

[19] R. Ellis, "On Some Fragments of Aeschylus and on the Suppliants," *Journal of Philology* 21 (1893), p. 30.
[20] Headlam's emendation.

Imagery of the *Suppliants*

ambiguous light, in the final lines of the play, as the chorus meaningfully pleads,

> May Zeus our lord avert cruel marriage with a hated husband, that very Zeus who delivered Io from torment by the strong embrace of his healing hand, making gracious his violence. (1062-7)

The might of Zeus's hand is a healing might, his strength beneficial. Touch and seizure, antithetical at first, are reconciled and synthesized at the end. More will be said later of the significance of the evolution of this image.

The imagery of breath, wind, and storm. The image develops from the aspect of the Io legend just discussed, and its evolution is similar to that of the image of touch and seizure. Like the latter, it is complex and subtle.

Preparation for it is made in the same lines which prepare for two of the other key images:

> Our race that boasts its birth from the gadfly-driven heifer at the touch and on-breathing of Zeus (16-18).

The conception of Epaphus resulted not only from the touch, but the "on-breathing" (ἐπίπνοια) of Zeus. *Epipnoia*, which in the usage of Plato usually denotes "inspiration," especially of the divine variety,[21] fre-

[21] Cf. *Laws*, 811c, and *Phaedrus*, 265b.

Imagery of the *Suppliants*

quently refers to wind rather than breath.[22] Aeschylus' use of the verbal form *epipnei* with Ares in *Seven Against Thebes*, 343, is good evidence of his awareness of the complexity of the word. In its occurrence here, it possesses only the denotation of *inspiratio*, but the range of the word varies as the drama progresses.

The basic meaning recurs in line 44, but not before a new element has been introduced into the image. That this element is a vital component of the figure may not appear entirely certain at first, but becomes increasingly so with the development of the play. The chorus prays to the gods in a hierarchy culminating in Zeus *sôtêr*—surely Zeus, the saviour of Io:

> receive as suppliants our band of women
> with the compassionate breeze [*pneumati*]
> of the land. (27-9)

The gentle *pneuma* desired by the Danaids is parallel to the *epipnoia* of Zeus. Plato makes no distinction between the two words, and appears to use them interchangeably[23]—*pneuma*, like *epipnoia*, can signify the divine *afflatus*. For the Egyptians, however, the chorus invokes no gentle *pneuma*:

> but for the teeming swarm of men of Aegyptus' race ... drive them back on the ocean—
> and there, when they meet with the stormsmiting [*cheimonotupoî*] whirlwind, the
> thunder and lightning, the rain-bearing

[22] Cf. Homer, *Iliad*, 5.698; Herodotus, 3.26; Theophrastus, *Vent.* 53.
[23] Cf. *Axiochus* 370c.

Imagery of the *Suppliants*

winds of the savage sea, may they perish (29-36).

This is the first full development of the image, which is thus prepared to oscillate among its three aspects; breath, wind, and storm.[24]

Wind and storm recur in 136-7, in close connection with Zeus:

> Our oars and our ship of wood, flax-girdled
> to withstand the sea, sped me with the help
> of gentle winds [*pnoiais*], stormless [*acheimaton*].
> Nor have I fault to find. But may the all-see-
> ing Father in due time afford a kindly end.
> (134-40)

Zeus is implied as the source of the gentle winds which brought the Danaids to Greece, and as a protector against storm.

Lines 166-7 abound with significant ambiguity. The chorus deplores the heavenly wrath that pursued Io, and says that it knows the fury of "wives [or husbands?] who rule in heaven," "for on a harsh wind [*pneumatos*] follows storm [*cheimôn*]." This passage doubtless denotes the wrath of Hera on discovery of Zeus's liaison with Io. The words *gametan ouranonikôn* are, however, indeterminate, and can connote "bridegrooms who conquer from heaven," as well as "brides who rule the heavens." Cannot the *pneuma*

---

[24] Sheppard observes a connection between two of the three aspects of this image, breath and storm (*op. cit.*, pp. 225-6). Hiltbrunner (*op. cit.*, pp. 17 and 31) perceives the relationship of all three aspects.

referred to here connote the *spiritus* of Zeus? The ephymnion is perhaps incurably corrupt, but the imagery of breath, wind, and storm is undoubtedly present, even if shadowed by intentional Aeschylean ambiguity. Storm follows on the heels of the harsh wind of Hera's wrath, and equally, perhaps, behind the on-breathing of Zeus; storm has overtaken the Danaids, the reincarnation of Io, and the last of a line conceived by the divine *afflatus*.

That this on-breathing is not to be considered altogether a gentle one is indicated by the words of the chorus, 576-8:

$$\beta\text{ί}\alpha\ \delta'\ \dot{\alpha}\pi\eta\mu\alpha\tau\sigma\sigma\theta\epsilon\nu\epsilon\hat{\iota}^{25}$$
$$\kappa\alpha\grave{\iota}\ \theta\epsilon\text{ί}\alpha\iota\varsigma\ \dot{\epsilon}\pi\iota\pi\nu\sigma\text{ί}\alpha\iota\varsigma$$
$$\pi\alpha\acute{\nu}\epsilon\tau\alpha\iota,$$

"By the harmless might of his violence and the divine on-breathing [her torment] is ended." The juxtaposition of *epipnoia* with *bia*, a strong word associated with physical assault, and with *sthenos* ("might"), supports the interpretation of the preceding image. The effects of the divine *epipnoia* were, of course, beneficial in the case of Io; the Danaids hope that "the all-contriver, Zeus of the fair wind" (594-5) will be as propitious for them.

The image recurs only once, near the end of the play. Its position is so emphatic, however—it appears in a passage which foreshadows action later in the trilogy—that one must concede its weight. The chorus, after honoring Aphrodite, turns to darker thoughts:

[25] Headlam's emendation.

Imagery of the *Suppliants*

But for the fugitives I fear the coming of
storms [*epipnoias*] of evil grief and bloody
wars. (1043-4)

Each previous occurrence of *epipnoia* has been in a
context which marks it plainly as the on-breathing of
Zeus. Where specific reference to wind and storm has
been desired, Aeschylus has consistently used *pneuma*,
anemos, and *cheimôn*. Yet here, where the context
patently calls for a word signifying strong winds or
storm, the poet creates an effective *paraprosdokian* by
employing *epipnoia*, much in the way he introduced
hrusion into the image of touch and seizure. The result
is a clever and subtle unification of the extended image
—which has varied in its shading from the divine
afflatus to the feared harsh wind of seizure by the
Egyptians and the tempest imprecated on the latter—
and a suggestive ambiguity. The Danaids fear not
only storm, but also the very *epipnoia* of Zeus![26]

The central imagery of the *Suppliants* differs mechanically from most other dramatic imagery. The
four key images all derive directly from a basic allegory, the Io legend. The forms assumed by Zeus and
Io furnish the point of departure for the bull-cow symbols. The general orientation of the legend—pursuer
and pursued, lover and beloved—suggests the male-
female contrast. The name Epaphus and the circumstances of his conception provide the basis for the

---

[26] Cf. Hiltbrunner, *op. cit.*, p. 31. Haupt's emendation,
epiploias, is gratuitous. I follow Turnebus; *epipnoias* is sensible
and closer to M's *epipnoiai*.

image of touch and seizure; the nature of conception performs the same function for the figure of breath, wind, and storm.

Not only do the key images derive from the central allegory, but they all serve to stress the vital significance of the allegory by referring the audience back and forth between the compared and the object of comparison; the reader is constantly reminded of the importance of the allegory for understanding of the drama. The images, moreover, serve to emphasize meaningful aspects of the allegory. They act as its interpreters, assist in clarification of its meaning, and foreshadow events to come. In short, the study of the machinery of imagery in the *Suppliants* is an indispensable avenue for penetration of the thought of the drama.

Can we be sure, however, that this imagery is intentionally developed in the manner described above, and that we are not "reading into" the play that which does not exist? The frequency and consistency of the imagery should provide an adequate answer to this question. None the less, it can reasonably be asked why certain portions of the play, notably the trimeters 176-203 and 980-1013, are totally devoid of key imagery. The explanation is that in both instances Danaus is the speaker, in virtual monologue. His attention, unlike that of his daughters, is not centered on their relationship to Io; he is their leader (*boularchos*), but they are the protagonist, and he does not, naturally, share their fiercely personal antagonism to the Egyptians, although he entertains his own strong

Imagery of the *Suppliants*

objections to them, however vaguely defined (cf. 227-8). The lack of Io imagery in the monologues of Danaus points up the peculiar relevance of that imagery to the maidens, and is thus a tribute to the care and consistency of Aeschylean composition.

It may also at first seem odd that the bulk of the key imagery occurs in roughly the first half of the drama. This apparent imbalance is explicable by the fact that the physical action of the drama is largely concentrated between the limits of the report by Danaus (710) and the debate between Pelasgus and the Herald (903-65); a profusion of imagery would retard the swift movement of these scenes. In addition, while the key images do not appear so frequently in the final choral songs as they do earlier in the play, each successive occurrence is increasingly significant and builds, as it were, on the substructure of the preceding imagery. The use of *epipnoia* in 1043, for example, is the capstone of all earlier imagery of breath, wind, and storm, and works in a synthetic capacity. Finally, there is every reason to suppose that the use of the four images was not interrupted by the end of the *Suppliants*, but that they continued to serve the poet well in the remaining plays of the trilogy.

There is, of course, much imagery in the *Suppliants* apart from the key imagery which I have analyzed. A considerable part of this imagery is merely characteristic of the poetic language, and not basically significant for the larger issues of the play. Metaphors of the sea occur frequently, as in 470-1,

Imagery of the *Suppliants*

> I have embarked upon a sea of ruin, fathomless, impassable, and nowhere is there a haven from evils.

but while such imagery is emotionally suggestive, it appears to be only typical of the tradition of Greek poetic expression, and by no means so vital for the interpretation of the *Suppliants* as the key imagery. It undergoes no consistent development, and is generally confined to the creation of momentary poetic effect.

Some use is made of animal symbolism. The Egyptians are characterized as *kynothraseis* ("insolent dogs," 758); Danaus replies:

> Yet the story goes that wolves are stronger than dogs. (760-1)

thus equating the Argives with the wolf, probably as a symbol of their protecting deity, the Apollo *Lykeios* of line 686.

The bird imagery of the *Suppliants* is rather more extensive.[27] The "hawk-pursued nightingale" (62) is surely the chorus, and the hawk the Egyptians; this assumption is confirmed by the words of Danaus:

> sit you on holy ground like a flock of doves
> in fear of hawks, of the same feathered tribe;
> kinsmen, but foes, who would pollute their race. How could bird devouring bird be pure? (223-6)

---

[27] Jean Dumortier, *Les Images dans La Poésie d'Eschyle* (Paris, 1935), pp. 1ff., sees the dove-hawk imagery as central in the *Suppliants*. Such images as that of the "winged ships" (734) are, however, poetic conventions.

Imagery of the *Suppliants*

a simile clear in its meaning. The image is employed again in 510:[28]

> Be sure we will not surrender you to the
> ravishing of winged creatures.

Later the Egyptians are characterized as ravens (751), birds of death rather than birds of prey. This new shading of imagery is nicely reiterated in the Danaids' suicide prayer:

> And then I shall not refuse to become a prey
> to dogs and a feast for the birds in the land.
> (800-1)

It is noticeable that this image recapitulates both dog and bird imagery; after death only will the Danaids surrender themselves to dogs and birds, established symbols of the Egyptians.

Such imagery, while it is poetically appropriate, and contributes to the emotional atmosphere, is of lesser importance in the larger context of the play. For interpretation of the drama, we must look instead into the meaning of the four key images, and the larger allegory which lies in back of them. That allegory, the Io legend, must be the next object of investigation.

[28] Cf. H. Mielke, *Die Bildersprāche des Aischylos* (Ohlau i. Schl., 1934), p. 76.

III. The Aeschylean Io

The legendary figure of Io exerted a singularly powerful attraction on the poet's imagination; not only does her story dominate the imagery of the *Suppliants*, but she also appears in the *Prometheus Bound* as the only human personnage in the play. No conclusions are justified on the basis of this possibly simple coincidence: the legend was not unfamiliar to the public[1] and was certainly fair material for the dramatist; it was, moreover, related to the matter of both plays, although somewhat more tenuously to that of the *Prometheus*. The scholar is, none the less, constrained to examine the role of Io and her story in the two tragedies, in order to ascertain whether this repeated

[1] The Io myth had been treated in epic poetry; how fully, it is difficult to say. Albert Severyns believes the theme was a secondary element of the *Aegimios*, a poem in the epic cycle ("Le Cycle Épique et l'Épisode d'Io," *Musée Belge* 30 [1926], pp. 119-30). Hesiod (fr. 47), Pindar, in *Nemean* 10.5 and *Pythian* 4.14, and Bacchylides (19) reveal an acquaintance with the legend. The latter part of the fifth century saw many literary references to Io: cf. the Euhemeristic account in Herodotus 1.1, which may derive from Hecataeus; the *Inachus* of Sophocles; Euripides' *Iphigeneia in Tauris* 394, *Phoenissae* 677 and 828, and *Suppliants* 628.9. This later popularity was undoubtedly in some measure a result of the influence of the Aeschylean plays. For a full list of references to the Io story, see Roscher, *Lexikon*, vol. 2, cols. 263-71, and Eitrem in *Real-Encyclopädie* 9[2] s.v. *Io*.

The Aeschylean Io

utilization of the legend[2] was only the result of coincidence.

I have touched on the structural significance of the Io allegory in the *Suppliants*. How important is her role in the *Prometheus*, where she participates as *dramatis persona*? It is not that of a dramatic pivot, but is none the less vital in its obvious function—that of assisting in the characterization of Zeus as an amoral tyrant, and of his reign as the rule of misanthropic, merciless, irresistible force. Secondarily, Io serves to increase our sympathy for Prometheus, the target of the tyrant's hatred. Still more important, however, is her less obvious function in the framework of the entire *Prometheia* trilogy. The release of Io from her woes is to provide the initial indication of the increasing wisdom of Zeus and the concomitant sowing of the seeds of compassion for humanity (848-52). The glory of her offspring Epaphus (850-2) is to be supplemented by the foundation of the royal Argive line (869); finally and climactically, her descendant Heracles is to free Prometheus (871-3), his act marking the coming of age of the divine wisdom and the synthesis of Promethean knowledge and humanitarianism with the effective Jovian power. Thus Io the persecuted becomes Io the glorious mother of national benefactors; her suffering is rewarded abundantly. The trilogy is a paean in honor of the Greek mind, but above all

[2] One must remember that the *Aegyptioi* and *Danaides* almost surely continued to employ the Io allegory, while the lost plays of the *Prometheia* very likely referred back to the story of Io in connection with her descendant Heracles.

The Aeschylean Io

an affirmation of the dignity of man and wise majesty of God, qualities attained through the perfecting course of evolution. Zeus the tyrant and Prometheus the forethinker coalesce in a compound slowly effected by the catalyst of *pathei mathos*.

Some scholars, it is true, reject this interpretation of the *Prometheia*, and have submitted the opinion that Prometheus is well-intentioned, but belies his name; he is incapable of understanding the mystery and sublimity of the Godhead and must, in the course of the trilogy, have been humbled and brought to realize the infallible perfection of Zeus. H. W. Smyth has effectively demonstrated a weakness of this position by pointing out that the important first moral impression of the reader of the *Prometheus* is of the justice of the Titan's cause;[3] such too, would have been the reaction of the Athenian audience, traditionally antagonistic to tyrants and oppressors.[4] It has been objected that such a despotic Zeus is not the Zeus of the *Suppliants* or the *Oresteia*. Obviously not. He is the primeval deity who is to evolve, in the course of many centuries, into the magnificent God of the latter plays.[5] Is there any foundation for the hypothesis that the emphatic use of the mythological figure of Io in both the *Prometheus* and the *Suppliants* indicates that these two tragedies were the product of the same period in the poet's career, and his fascination with the story of the horned

[3] *Op. cit.*, p. 109.
[4] Cf. Thomson, *op. cit.*, pp. 320-6.
[5] Cf. Smyth, *op. cit.*, pp. 115-6. H.D.F. Kitto, in his *Form and Meaning in Drama* (London, 1956), pp. 69-86, supports this interpretation at length.

The Aeschylean Io

maiden was a result of his preoccupation with a certain problem at a particular stage of his dramatic development? A few years ago, the majority of scholars would undoubtedly have retorted in the negative; the *Suppliants* was almost universally considered the earliest drama in European literature, while the *Prometheus* was generally assigned a considerably later date. A recently published papyrus has changed the picture, and the evidence supporting an earlier date for the *Suppliants* is far from conclusive;[6] conversely, there is evidence which suggests that chronological proximity of the two plays is not only possible but probable. This evidence rests on inspection of certain common elements of verbal detail and content.

Similarities of conception, imagery, and verbal detail conduce to the belief that the two dramas belong to the same period, or that the poet wrote the second with vivid reminiscence of the earlier. These similarities are to be found in the account of the end of Io's wanderings and the story of the Danaids told by Prometheus, which so resemble the story and idiom of the *Suppliants* that one might almost call them a very free *cento*. The very length of the account—twenty-five lines—is far greater than is necessary for purposes of plot, and serves notice that the story of the Danaids strongly attracted the poet at the time of the composition of the *Prometheus*.

An examination of some of these similarities may be informative. Prometheus prefaces his account of the end of the Io story with the remark

[6] See Appendix A.

The Aeschylean Io

The rest I shall tell to you and her together, returning to the same track as that of my former tale (τῶν πάλαι λόγων ἴχνος, 844-5).

The use of *ichnos* ("track") in connection with the myth of Io recalls to us the words of the Danaids,

> παλαιὸν δ' εἰς ἴχνος μετέσταν,
> ματέρος ἀνθονόμους ἐπωπάς (538-9)
> I have come to the ancient track of my mother, to the place where she was watched while she grazed on flowers.

The occurrence of *palaion* and *palai*, in close proximity to *ichnos* in both cases, appears highly suggestive; the possibility of simple coincidence is lessened by *Suppliants* 1017, where the chorus avers that

> ἴχνος τὸ πρόσθεν οὐ διαστρέψω φρενός.
> I will not swerve from the former track of my purpose.

The meaning and function of *prosthen* in this line is equivalent to that of *palaion* and *palai* in the other passages.

The offspring of Epaphus, Libya, is described in the *Suppliants* as

> megiston gês . . . karpoumenê (317)
> reaping the fruits of the greatest expanse of the earth.

while Prometheus predicts to Io:

The Aeschylean Io

you shall give birth to Epaphus the dark
one, who will reap the fruits [*karpôsetai*] of
all the land watered by the broad-flowing
Nile. (851-2)

The repetition of a root of *karp-* in almost identical context cannot be ascribed to chance alone.

Aeschylus, in the *Prometheus* as well as the *Suppliants*, expressed the male-female contrast inherent in the Danaid myth.[7] The Danaids are termed a *genna pentêkontapais . . . thêlusporos* ("race of fifty daughters of woman's seed") (*Prometheus* 853-5); the Egyptians are received in Argos with *thêluktonoî Arei* ("woman-dealt slaughter," 860-1), when "each bride will rob her husband of life." (862)

Effective use is made in the *Prometheus* of imagery of the cow; such imagery appears even in the cosmic cataclysm of the final scene, when Io is no longer on stage. As C. M. Dawson has shown, such terms as *paramukatai* ("bellows in answer"), here applied to the violent turmoil of the elements, link the torment of the Io cow to the distress of Prometheus.[8] The hawk-dove imagery of the *Suppliants*[9] is also closely paralleled by *Prometheus*, 856-9:

They, with hearts aflame like hawks in close
chase of doves, will come in pursuit of a
marriage that should not be pursued

---
[7] See above, pp. 27-31.
[8] "Notes on the Final Scene of *Prometheus Vinctus*," *Classical Philology* 46 (1951), pp. 237-9.
[9] See above, p. 44.

The Aeschylean Io

These similarities might appear to support the older chronological view, yet their occurrence may well be the product of almost contemporary composition of the tragedies. Such chronological proximity is made more probable by the indisputable community of content of the two plays. The entire dramatic situation of the *Suppliants* is based on a theological conception not assumed, but developed, in the *Prometheia*. This conception is intimately involved with the symbol of Io.

Io is characterized in the *Suppliants* as a woman who has endured great agony, but has been amply rewarded by her introduction into a state of ineffable happiness as the result of the conception of Epaphus; the Danaids dwell on the glory of Io's release from torment rather than the torment itself. Consequently, the Danaids emphasize the role of Hera as the instigator of Io's woes, while Zeus is appealed to as the God of justice and compassion who permits no wrong to go unpunished. These conceptions obviously conflict, for the mighty deity whose very thought is action fulfilled[10] cannot be conceived of as allowing a lesser god to inflict harsh punishment on an innocent mortal. As I will try to show later, a consistent characteristic of the Danaids is their ability to understand partially, but failure to comprehend fully the significance of human and divine motives in past and present. Partial understanding is revealed in the sonorous words of the first choral ode:

[10] Cf. lines 101-3.

The Aeschylean Io

> But may Zeus grant that in all truth it go
> well with us. The desire of Zeus is hard to
> track out; truly, it flashes everywhere, even
> in the darkness, but with issue obscure to
> mortals.
> It falls safely, and not on its back, whatever
> is decreed for fulfillment by the nod of Zeus.
> For dark and tangled stretch the paths of his
> mind, unseen by our vision. (86-95)[11]

But the chorus does not understand that their words apply accurately to the fortunes of Io, as well as their own. The desire of Zeus is not only his wish, but also his lust for Io; Io's lot was indeed obscure until her arrival in Egypt. The deep but unconscious feeling that Zeus, not Hera, was responsible for Io's torment is revealed strikingly through repeated amphibolies.[12]

In the *Prometheus*, the wrath of Hera is subordinated to the guilt of Zeus, the enemy of humanity. The glory of Io's future is rather cryptically predicted by Prometheus; he cannot predict it emphatically without weakening his own position as the sympathetic victim of a cruel deity. Aeschylus was on the horns of a dramatic dilemma—as the possessor of prophetic powers, Prometheus must know that Zeus will, some time in the future, become a merciful deity; dramatically, he cannot admit this.

It is believed by many that, in the course of the *Prometheia*, the young divine tyrant becomes the just, wise, compassionate God known to us from the *Ores-*

[11] I follow Smyth's text.   [12] See below, pp. 65-8.

teia.[13] The beginning of this change is marked by the restoration of Io to human form, and her deliverance from suffering. The *Suppliants*, on the other hand, does not refer directly to this evolution of the Godhead, but appears to accept it categorically as an accomplished fact. The Zeus who unleashed the torrent of Io's woes (the persecutor Hera is no more than one aspect of the primitive Zeus) has fulfilled the promise of development symbolized by the release of Io, which manifests his reconciliation with mankind, and has thus become a god of wisdom and justice. Io, in both plays, is a symbol of man's sorrows and man's hopes.

In view of these facts, two interpretations are permissible. Either the *Suppliants* was written later than the *Prometheus*, with the thesis of the latter still fresh in the poet's mind, or it was composed in the same period as the *Prometheus*, and both plays were based on the same theological hypothesis expressed through similar legendary symbols;[14] It is, I believe, not possible to determine which of these hypotheses is correct. Even were it possible to do so, the result would not be of the greatest moment. What is important is the conclusion that the *Suppliants* and the *Prometheus*, based on identical theological doctrine, cannot be fully interpreted independently of each other, especially

[13] See pp. 47-8 and note 5 above. For a recent example of the minority view, see H. Lloyd-Jones, "Zeus in Aeschylus," *Journal of Hellenic Studies* 76 (1956), pp. 55-67.

[14] It is, of course, possible but hardly probable, that Aeschylus adhered strictly to the same theological belief conveyed by the same symbols, without alteration, for some twenty years, the period demanded by the traditional dating of the two plays.

The Aeschylean Io

since each play formed the first member of an otherwise lost trilogy.

The meaning of the allegory of Io in the *Suppliants*, and consequently the meaning of the tragedy itself, can, I believe, be unveiled by means of its interpretation in the light of the *Prometheus*. In the discussion which follows, I shall endeavor to establish this interpretation and to demonstrate its detailed application in the text of the *Suppliants*.

IV. The Meaning of the Motif of Io

THE recurrent comparison of the Danaids to Io, effected directly and through allegory and other imagery, cannot be the simple comparison accepted in the traditional interpretations of the *Suppliants*. It would have been both naïve and pointless for the poet to persist in reminding his audience that the maidens are fugitives, and are therefore like their ancestress, who was also a fugitive; such aimless superficiality is certainly not Aeschylean. Closer investigation will, I believe, reveal that the *Prometheus* holds the key to a complex and deeply meaningful allegorical structure which is central to the interpretation of the *Suppliants*.

The point of departure of the allegorical comparison is, undoubtedly, the fact that both the Danaids and Io are fugitives; this slight and external resemblance affords, however, no insight whatsoever into the meanings of the drama. More significant is the similarity between the motives behind the flight of Io and that of the sisters. The Danaids flee to Argos to escape the unwelcome advances of their suitors; Io's flight, too, is caused by the lust of a suitor. In the *Prometheus*, as we have seen, Zeus is held accountable for the flight of Io, and indirectly so in the *Suppliants*.[1] Con-

[1] Cf. Ch. III.

Meaning of the Motif

sequently, it may seem that the poet wishes to tell us that the actions of the Danaids—the pursued—may be clarified by comparison with Io, and that the motives of the Egyptians—the pursuers—must be interpreted in the light of the character of Zeus.

Those who would accept the comparison of the Danaids and Io as valid (because Aeschylus makes it quite plain that such a comparison is intended) might none the less object to the assumption of a parallel between the Egyptians and Zeus.[2] The existence of the parallel can, however, be demonstrated through close analysis of the tragedy; it is subordinate to the major comparison, but still perfectly apparent. Basically, of course, it exists by implication. If the Danaids and Io are alike because their flight is caused by a suitor's lust, then a relationship is automatically established between the suitors of each; we may say that desire and effective power are the relating characteristics.[3] It might, however, be objected that such a relationship is an accidental by-product of the allegory, and that the poet hoped to limit the application of the allegory to the comparison of the Danaids and Io.

[2] Gilbert Murray is an exception. He observes that Io's function is "chiefly to deepen the issue; to show that these women are not the first who have had to face the same trial. Their ancestress Io was pursued in the same way by Zeus himself." (*op. cit.*, p. 36).

[3] Zeus does not, of course, pursue Io literally; the gadfly sent by Hera pursues her. But Zeus is the cause of her pursuit, through the sequence of events set in motion by his lust. Cf. *Prometheus*, 737-8, "For Zeus, desiring to lie with this maiden, has imposed on her these wanderings." Hera is, moveover, only an aspect of the deity.

Meaning of the Motif

This objection can be met by reference to the imagery, which reveals that the Zeus-Egyptian comparison is intentional and strongly stressed—for example, the image of touch and seizure clearly draws a parallel between the violence of the Egyptians and the imposition on Io of the will of Zeus. The parallel is further emphasized by the choral words of the first stasimon, where the Egyptians are described as "possessing in their mad intent an inescapable goad (*kentron*) (109-10)." The *kentron* is not only the goad of passion which impels the Egyptians to the pursuit; it is also the inescapable gadfly which follows close behind the Danaids, as it had behind Io. In the case of the former, it represents the Egyptians; in the latter, the result of the actions of Zeus.

It is, of course, true that the comparison of the Egyptians and the Zeus of the *Suppliants* and *Oresteia* cannot be pressed very far—but the Zeus of the *Oresteia* is not the *only* Zeus of the *Suppliants*. In both the *Prometheus* and the *Suppliants*, the ruler of the gods owns a double character. The Promethean Zeus is not only the deity of the extant play, a new tyrant whose servants are Power and Force, and who wishes to annihilate mankind; he is also the Zeus of a future age who, having freed Io from suffering, will recognize the release of Prometheus by Heracles, and become reconciled with the friend of man. Conversely with the *Suppliants*. The god of the play, appealed to as a god of wisdom, justice, and compassion, is also the Zeus of the past, whose lust and brutality were

Meaning of the Motif

responsible for Io's torment.[4] The Zeus of the future in the *Prometheus* is the contemporary Zeus of the *Suppliants*; the Zeus of the past in the *Suppliants* is the present Zeus of the *Prometheus*.

Consequently, the comparison of the Egyptians with only *one aspect* of Zeus seems complete; they are like the Zeus who caused Io's flight. What then of the equation of the Danaids and Io? Like that of the Egyptians and Zeus, it appears to be incomplete. The Danaids murdered their husbands; Io, at length, submitted to hers, and gave birth to a ruling hero. Thus the Aeschylean allegory apparently suffers from the defect of an awkward limitation.

We possess, however, very substantial evidence that this un-Aeschylean imperfection owes its existence only to the loss of the *Egyptians* and *Danaids*. In the *Suppliants*, the Danaids are a single minded, unified group of sisters who act as one person (although, as we shall see, strong intimations of an impending dissension are present in the final scene), nor are the Egyptians characterized as individuals. This unity of character, purpose, and action is not, however, typical of the story of the remainder of the trilogy; in fact, the dissolution of this unity was very probably a primary theme of the final play.[5] Not all the Danaids

[4] Cf. H. Bogner, "Die Stellung des Zeus im *Prometheus Desmotês*," *Philologus* 87 (1932), p. 470. He observes that there are two "Zeuses" in the *Suppliants*: "Schon in den Hiketiden bezeichnet das Wort Zeus zweierlei, einmal den Gott des Mythos, der als Stier die Kuh bespringt (299), und dann die vollkommenste Macht überhaupt (etwa 524f.)."

[5] See below, Ch. V.

Meaning of the Motif

kill their husbands, nor do all the Egyptians deserve such a death. The exceptions are Hypermnestra and Lynceus. Hypermnestra, far more than the other sisters, resembles Io. We may assume that she shares with her sisters, at first, the repugnance to the male typical of Io, but unlike the other maidens, her resemblance to Io does not stop at this point. Like Io, Hypermnestra finally understands the full meaning of her destiny, and she refuses to murder her husband. What motive leads her to this understanding? Fortunately, a passage from the *Prometheus* supplies the answer to this question. It is the realization of the glory and necessity of motherhood, the perhaps not fully conscious realization of the role of the female as the transmitter of life and civilization:

> But one of them the desire for offspring[6]
> shall charm so as not to slay her bedmate,
> and her resolve shall be blunted. For, from
> the choice before her, she shall prefer to be
> called coward rather than murderess.
>
> (865-8)

Further support for this interpretation is provided by the recurrent reference to fertility and motherhood in the imagery of the *Suppliants*, especially in the choral benediction of Argos.[7]

---

[6] A few scholars (cf. H. W. Smyth's translation) hold that *paidôn* should be construed with *mian* rather than with *himeros*; but cf. E. Harrison, "Hypermnestra," *Proceedings of the Cambridge Philological Society*, 160-2 (1935), p. 8. He points out that the caesura decides against such a construction.

[7] See Ch. V. Méautis, *op. cit.*, pp. 67 and 70, emphasizes

Meaning of the Motif

The motive supplied by Aeschylus for the action of Hypermnestra becomes even more significant when it is realized that he was evidently confronted with a choice within the tradition of the myth, or else departed from the established version. Both Apollodorus (2.1.5) and the scholiast to Pindar (*Nemean* 10.10) inform us that Hypermnestra spared Lynceus because he did not violate her virginity. Quite a different story from that given by Aeschylus! And hardly compatible with the tradition that Hypermnestra gave birth to the first prince of the royal Argive line.[8] Accordingly, Aeschylus chose or created a version more consonant with both the tradition and one of the principal theses of the trilogy, the importance of fertility and motherhood.

Hypermnestra's motive thus forges a final link in the bond between herself and Io. Both finally accept their suitors, and both give birth to kings; Io to Epaphus, Hypermnestra to Abas;[9] both are glorified in the foundation or continuation of the divinely-descended line that will rule Argos and culminate in Heracles the savior and the wise Cadmus. Both learn to accept their destiny, unlike the forty-nine Danaids (or forty-eight, if we except Amymone), who are abnormally blind to destiny.

We may assume that the case of Lynceus paralleled that of Hypermnestra. As co-founder of the royal

---

the theme of motherhood in the trilogy, and calls attention to the existence of this theme in the *Agamemnon*, *Persians*, and *Niobe* (pp. 59-60).

[8] Cf. *Prometheus*, 869; Apollodorus, 2.2.1.

[9] Cf. Apollodorus, *ibid*.

Meaning of the Motif

house, he cannot be as evil as the other Egyptians are characterized in the *Suppliants*, through the biased reports of the chorus and through the medium of their representative, the herald (note how like the use of Kratos, Bia, and Hermes to characterize Zeus, is the function of the herald in the characterization of the Egyptians!). Danaus himself informs us that "an unknown company is tested by time" (993). Probably, as with Zeus and Io, Aeschylus described Lynceus' violent pursuit of the Danaids as climaxing in a more gentle, compassionate treatment of Hypermnestra. Such a portrayal is quite logical, and would be necessary to complete the application of the Io allegory to the Danaid myth. There is good reason to suppose that Aeschylus would feel such completion to be aesthetically desirable.

In consequence, the preliminary formula, which may be stated as

$$\text{Zeus : Io = Egyptians : Danaids}$$

is proved incomplete and must be revised. It is, however, valid in the equation of the Egyptians to the contemporary Zeus of the *Prometheus Bound* (not to the god to whom the Danaids pray) and in the similarity of the Danaids' flight to that of Io; therefore, the second hypothesis,

$$\text{Zeus : Io = Lynceus : Hypermnestra}$$

is not by itself altogether adequate. Only when the two hypotheses are synthesized can the allegory be fully

Meaning of the Motif

explained and the imagery of the play understood. The allegory can now be diagrammed as follows:

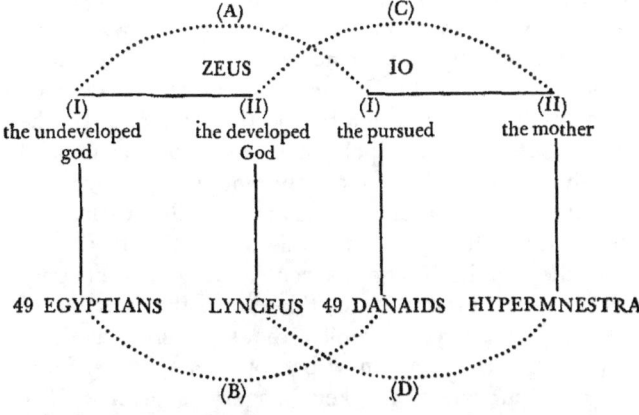

The perfect balance of the allegory is apparent. The relationship of the primitive Zeus with Io the pursued (A) is parallel to that of the Egyptians and the Danaids (B); the circumstances of Zeus's final courtship of Io (C) are closely similar to those involving Lynceus and Hypermnestra (D). Nor is the allegory limited to the comparison of relationships: the character of Zeus (I) explains the actions of the Egyptians; Io (I) is like the Danaids, and Io (II) like Hypermnestra. The comparison of Zeus (II) and Lynceus was perhaps not made explicit, but Lynceus was, at all events, subordinate to Hypermnestra as a focal point of interest.

It is evident, then, that the Io imagery of the *Suppliants* is not a simple, prosaic comparison of the flight

Meaning of the Motif

of the maidens and their ancestress, but a complex, perfectly evolved parallel which stands at the center of the meaning of the entire trilogy. Aeschylus had access to two more or less popular myths which exhibited a few superficial similarities; his creative genius molded them, in the *Prometheus* and the *Suppliants*, into an intricately beautiful poetic structure. In the *Suppliants*, the principal poetic effect is one created by the tension arising from the now symphonic, now apparently discordant application of the varied aspects of the Io myth to the tale of the Danaids. Both the allegory itself and its contributory key imagery assist in the production of this effect; the function of the key imagery, of which the structure has been analyzed earlier, may now be appreciated more fully.

The function of the key imagery is diverse. The bull-cow and male-female images may be described as allusive and concentrative; by virtue of their direct relationship to the Io myth, they serve to point up the importance of the Io allegory, and their very frequent recurrence focuses the mind of the audience on the allegory. They effect, however, little explanation of the applicability of the Io theme to the Danaids (beyond emphasizing the universality of the forces involved). The images of touch and seizure, and breath, wind and storm, on the other hand, may be termed exegetic, although they too exert the effect of concentration. Since they possess this explanatory force, they are, of course, more vital vehicles of meaning than the simpler imagery.

These two exegetic images afford us much insight

Meaning of the Motif

into the deeper significance of the Io allegory. They explain how the situation of the Danaids is parallel to the legend of Io, and contribute to the tension rising from the conflict between the partial understanding of the Danaids and the fuller knowledge possessed by the audience. These functions of the exegetic imagery can be demonstrated by brief examination of the text.

First, the image of touch and seizure. The chorus announces in the first stasimon (having hinted at it earlier, in line 17) that their ancestor Epaphus was conceived by Io at the touch (and on-breathing) of Zeus (40-47). This reference paves the way for the development of the image. 313-15 expand its scope by the use of the word *hrusion*, which introduces ambiguity into the previously colorless *ephapsis*; the caress of Io by Zeus now connotes both gentleness and violence. Pelasgus' warning, "that strife may not seize on you for prize" (*hrusiôn ephapsetai*, 412), containing, as it does, the two key words, and applying them to the Danaids instead of to Io, now completes the image. The touch of Zeus is compared (by the poet, not by Pelasgus) to the touch of the Egyptians; the aspect of violence is here emphasized. The Danaids themselves pick up this thread a few lines later, as they beg Pelasgus, "see me not seized [*hrusiastheisan*] from this sanctuary of many gods" (423-4). Their ironic half understanding is displayed in their prayer to Zeus for deliverance (524-99). They call on him to destroy their suitors, the Egyptians (528-30), then immediately thereafter ask him in his capacity as *ephaptôr Ious* to recall the tale of Io (533-5) —which

Meaning of the Motif

culminated in the very fate they hope to avoid, that of submission to a lover![10] The happy effects of Zeus's caress (Io's release from torment and the birth of the wondrous Epaphus) are then described by the maidens (576-89), but despite their atavistic tendencies, they cannot understand the true applicability of the story of Io to their own lot. It is this partial, incomplete understanding which creates the tragic conflict in the character of the Danaids. The bitter irony of the situation is climaxed in the lovely choral words:

> To what god should I appeal with greater reason, for the just deeds he has wrought? Himself our father and lord, sower of our seed with his own hand, mighty builder of our race, old in wisdom, the all-contriver, Zeus of the fair wind. (590-5)

The Danaids ask to whom they should more properly plead for deliverance from their pursuers than to Zeus —the god who was responsible for the flight of Io, and who delivered her from her woes only after an enforced "marriage"!

The full meaning of the image of touch and seizure is developed in the final strophe of the *Suppliants*. Again they pray to Zeus,

> May Zeus our lord avert cruel marriage with a hated husband, that very Zeus who delivered Io from torment by the strong em-

[10] Thomson, *op. cit.*, p. 300, perceives the irony of this prayer.

Meaning of the Motif

> brace of his healing hand, making gracious
> his violence. (1062-7)[11]

Zeus is invoked to avert the impending marriage with the Egyptians. He is implored to do this in his capacity as the god who released Io from torment by the benevolent strength of his generative caress. The result of his action, the chorus implies, was a positive good. But the maidens do not realize that completion of their comparison with Io requires that they marry the Egyptians—or rather, only one of them comes to this realization. Hypermnestra understands her destiny of motherhood, accepts the caress of Lynceus, and like Io, gives birth to a ruler. Touch and seizure are synthesized, the tension of the image resolved.

The imagery of breath, wind, and storm functions in much the same way. Like the preceding image, it is at first unambiguous, and signifies the divine *afflatus* instrumental in the conception of Epaphus (17 and 44); however, it soon acquires multiple suggestion, its meaning including not only the *afflatus* but calm wind (28) and storm (33-6). The tension of the image then develops from the conflict of its three aspects.

In 576-8,

> By the harmless might of his violence[12] and
> the divine on-breathing [her torment] is
> ended

---

[11] Cf. *Choephoroe*, 1059-60, for the construction of the final phrase.
[12] Reading, with Headlam, *biai d'apēmatosthenei*.

Meaning of the Motif

the conflict is especially apparent. As the touch of Zeus is both caress and seizure, so his on-breathing is characterized as both gentle and violent. The final use of the image is especially significant. The chorus announces, near the end of the play,

> But for the fugitives I fear the coming of storms [*epipnoias*] of evil grief and bloody wars. (1043-4)

Epipnoia, used previously to denote the divine *afflatus* or gentle wind, must here signify violent storm. The chorus thus states that it fears not only the storm of grief and war, but specifically the lot of marriage with the Egyptians; the sexual aspect of *epipnoia* is appropriated to a different context, and completes the linking of the figure with Zeus and the allegory of Io.

The key imagery forms an integral part of the structure of the allegory, but only a part. The other references to Io are also illuminating, and deserve analysis in the light of the conclusions thus far drawn. These references, like the key images, are of two types, of unequal importance to the critic. The less important are those references which are allusive or concentrative; they state primarily that a similarity exists between the past or present situation of the Danaids and the legend of Io and Zeus. As an example of this type, the metaphorical comparison of the maidens to a lost heifer (the Io heifer) may be cited.[13] Such metaphor may imply, but does not explicitly indicate the va-

[13] Cf. above, p. 26.

Meaning of the Motif

lidity of further comparison; it affords, therefore, relatively limited insight into the thought of the trilogy.

The majority of the references are, in varying degree, exegetic. For purposes of analysis, they may be subdivided into two (not entirely distinct) classes: (1) those explanatory images which not only state the existence of past and present similarity between the Danaids and Io, but clarify it in greater or less detail, casting light on motives and character; (2) those prophetic images which strongly foreshadow similarity between the future of the Danaids and the Io legend.

The Danaids' atavistic obsession that they are, in some sense, a reincarnation of Io, is a determining and dominant element of their character. Yet their perception of similarity between themselves and Io is woefully limited and superficial; the first stasimon reveals this. The sisters call on their ancestor Epaphus, enjoining him to save them from the fate of enforced marriage with the Egyptians, ignoring the pertinence of the fact that Epaphus himself was the issue of the enforced union of Io and Zeus. They are sometimes conscious only of Io's torments as precedent of their lot:

> now in the pasturing places of my ancient
> mother, recalling her labors of old (50-2)

and not of the "happy ending" of her story. This half sight which characterizes the maidens is strongly reemphasized in a number of Zeus-Io images; in these instances, the Danaids appear to be aware of Zeus only

Meaning of the Motif

as the deity who released Io from her sufferings, and not as the god who was initially responsible for them. Zeus will be blamed for dishonoring the "child" of his own union by force, if he fails to prevent the repetition of such a union (168-74). Danaus asks his daughters,

> How could bird devouring bird be pure?
> And how could man be pure, who would
> wed a bride unwilling, taken from an un-
> willing father? (226-8)

yet it surely does not occur to either that Zeus should not be considered pure, if subject to judgment by the same standard. The Danaids' mental confusion even leads them to appeal to Zeus to release them from torment as he did Io,

> Looking with favor on our race of women
> old in story, recall the happy tale of our
> ancestress, the woman dear to you. (531-4)

their curiously warped understanding preventing them from perceiving that such a release implies submission to the male and motherhood.[14] How does Aeschylus explain the existence of this strange mental limitation? Not because the Danaids are obsessed by thoughts of palingenesis, since these, if properly extended, would endow them with correct insight. Human limitations are, of course, a contributing factor, and are expressed as such by the chorus:

> How should I contemplate the mind of Zeus,
> a boundless sight? (1057-8)

[14] This image is, of course, ironically prophetic.

Meaning of the Motif

> For dark and tangled stretch the paths of
> his mind, unseen by our vision. (93-5)

Most important, however, is the fact that the Danaids appear to be afflicted by a madness[15] like that suffered by Io, a madness that will not allow them to see life in its proper proportions. No literal gadfly maddens them, but it exists none the less in the person of the Egyptians, who are described as "possessing in their mad intent an inescapable goad" (109-10). They have followed, these descendants of the cow maiden, in "Io's tracks" to the extent of affliction by partial insanity:

> I have come to the ancient track of my
> mother, to the place where she was watched
> while she grazed on flowers, the rich pasturage whence Io, driven on by the gadfly,
> fled in madness (538-42)

Also, as with Io, the root of their disease is an aversion to marriage, symbolized by the goddess Hera:

> Maddened by ignoble toils and frenzied by
> the torturing goad of Hera. (562-4)

Whether this aversion is general or specific is, I believe, quite immaterial; there is never (in the *Suppliants*) any suggestion of marriage of the Danaids to others than the Egyptians. The fact is that the

---

[15] Walter Nestle observes signs of madness in the threat by the chorus to commit suicide on the altars (*Menschliche Existenz und Politische Erziehung in der Tragödie des Aischylos*, Stuttgart, 1934, p. 17).

Meaning of the Motif

Egyptians want to marry the Danaids, the Danaids reject their advances, and the latter are maddened (as, symbolically, was Io) at the prospect of this union, a union which (in the case of Hypermnestra, like Io) could be productive of positive good.

The madness of the Danaids is further confirmed by the comparison of their frantic desire to escape, and their expressed wish for self-destruction, to similar emotions experienced by Io in the *Prometheus*. First, their turbidly voiced longings, shadowed alike with overtones of darkness and death:

> Alas, land of the cow, revered in all justice, what will befall us? Where in this Apian land shall we flee—is there anywhere some dark hiding place? Would that I might become the black smoke that nears the clouds of Zeus, soaring like wingless dust, to perish invisible, unseen. (*Suppliants*, 776-82)

> Consume me in fire, or hide me in the earth, or give me to the jaws of the monsters of the deep (*Prometheus*, 582-3)

The death wish itself is expressed in similar mood and terms:

> Would that I might find somewhere in upper air a seat against which the watery clouds become snow, or some bare crag—sheer, beyond sight, in solitary thought, beetling, the haunt of vultures—to bear witness to my abysmal fall. (*Suppliants*, 792-7)

Meaning of the Motif

> For death is freedom from laments and ills.
> May my doom come to me, before the marriage-bed. What remedy may I yet find to
> deliver me from wedlock?[16] (*Suppliants*, 802-7)

> What profit for me then in life? Why do I
> not hurl myself from this jagged rock, so
> that dashed to earth, I might have freedom
> from all my woes? For better to die once
> and for all, than to suffer all one's days.
> (*Prometheus*, 747-51)

In summary, the Io imagery affords us great insight into the character of the Danaids, who have allowed their hatred of a group of suitors to derange them and shock from them all sense of proportion. The murder later in the trilogy is a logical consequence of their mental state, just as suicide would be.[17] There is no need to visualize the sisters as a band of warrior maidens or Amazons in order to justify the psychology of the murder.

The prophetic Io imagery performs the function of foreshadowing events to occur in the *Egyptians* and *Danaids*; more important, it provides one of the keys to correct interpretation of the trilogy, since in some cases it foreshadows not only events but the development of motives and character.

The continuing applicability of the allegory of Io

---

[16] Reading, with M, *temno* in 807. Cf. *Agamemnon* 17 for this image (which resists translation) of compounding therapeutic herbs. Cf. *Prometheus* 606.

[17] Cf. Méautis, *op. cit.*, pp. 57-8.

Meaning of the Motif

is stressed in several of these passages. The Danaids announce:

> Now in the pasturing places of my ancient mother, recalling her labors of old, I shall present trustworthy tokens to those who dwell in the land; and other signs, though unforeseen, shall yet appear. And men will come to know the truth of my words. (50-6)

Lines 55 and 56 clearly refer in prospect to further similarities (and perhaps dissimilarities) between the legend of Io and the fate of the maidens. Later, the chorus assures Danaus that

> Unless the gods have devised something unforeseen, I will not swerve from the former track of my purpose. (1016-7)

These words denote that the Danaids will not swerve from their established resolve, but they also convey an importantly different connotation. The sisters will not depart from the track of Io;[18] the marriage of the fifty and perhaps the fate of Hypermnestra are foreshadowed.

The marriage is also foreshadowed dimly when the Danaids' confidence descends to its nadir:

> Fear and dread enfold me, lest my far-coursed flight has truly been of no avail. Father, I perish with terror. (736-8)

They fear that their flight from the male, like Io's

[18] Cf. line 538.

Meaning of the Motif

wanderings, may have been futile. The clearest predictions of marriage, however, are conveyed through the key imagery previously discussed.

The murder of the Egyptians is also prophesied through the imagery of Io, most significantly in the ambiguous words of Danaus, as he requests Pelasgus to supply him with a bodyguard:

> For the Nile rears a breed unlike that of
> Inachus. Beware lest boldness beget fear.
> For, ere now, men have slain friends
> [*philous*] through ignorance. (497-9)

Ostensibly, he means only that his life and that of his daughters are endangered by their outlandish appearance. The choice of words, however, is highly suggestive; Inachus was not only an Argive river, but the father of Io. When this relationship to the Io allegory is perceived, Danaus' statement becomes meaningfully ambiguous—to paraphrase, "The Danaids are *not* like Io (i.e., submissive); beware lest overconfidence give birth to fear, for murder of loved ones (e.g., husbands?) has occurred before through ignorance (of their true nature)." The real cause of the murder—the selfish limitation of the Danaids' vision—is thus cryptically predicted.

The most significant foreshadowing is, however, conveyed through the structure of the entire allegory, not its subsidiary elements. It informs us that the Danaids are maddened and blinded, like the Io of the *Prometheus*; that one of them regains her vision and recognizes the responsibilities of motherhood, and

Meaning of the Motif

that she receives due reward for her superior understanding of destiny. There now remains the task of examining the compatibility of these conclusions with other internal and external evidence, and of attempting to reconstruct, as far as possible, the meaning of the Danaid trilogy.

V. Hypermnestra and the Themes of the Trilogy

A FORBIDDING challenge confronts the critic who attempts the reconstruction of the plots of the *Egyptians* and the *Danaids*. The thinness of our evidence demands unusual caution in any effort to recreate the broader outlines of those two plays, let alone the details of the action; even if some fortunate scholar should intuit the true facts, he would find himself, like Gorgias, unable to communicate earnestly his conclusions to others. In consequence, this summary contains no new hypothesis concerning the action of the lost plays of the trilogy, and deals with possibilities of plot only to the extent necessary to demonstrate that the conclusions I have drawn are compatible with the more or less solid facts offered by our tradition.

While much use has been made, in attempts at the reconstruction of the trilogy, of evidence other than that found in the *Suppliants*, such evidence is, in fact, extremely tenuous. We possess many accounts of the Danaid myth, but the treatment of the legend by other authors bears no necessary relation to the account Aeschylus followed or created; the freedom of the tragic poet is well attested by Euripides' use or creation of conflicting versions of the myth of Iphigeneia and by the divergent treatment of the Philocte-

Hypermnestra and the Themes

tes legend by the three tragic dramatists. On the other hand, we are justified in placing much more reliance on the brief story of the Danaids given by Aeschylus in the *Prometheus* (853-69), since there is no apparent reason why this account should differ materially from the plot of the lost plays. Unfortunately, the treatment of the myth in the *Prometheus* furnishes only the barest outline of the story, but does emphasize three events: the murder of the Egyptians, the disobedience of Hypermnestra, and her foundation of the royal Argive line. This emphasis argues for the validity of the conclusion, drawn from the Io allegory, that Hypermnestra must have played a most important role in the trilogy.

The fragments of the lost plays, with one exception, offer little assistance; only the speech of Aphrodite (fragment 44) can be considered significantly informative, and it has been variously interpreted.[1] However, its principal theme, the description of the speaker as the first cause of fertility, is obviously thoroughly consonant with the emphasis given to motherhood in the Io allegory. It would, therefore, serve exceedingly well as a speech delivered in behalf of Hypermnestra.

The *Suppliants* contains some foreshadowing—beyond that directly connected with the Io allegory—of the action of the later plays. The murder of the Egyptians is probably predicted when the Danaids announce they have come as suppliants,

[1] Cf. above, p. 12.

Hypermnestra and the Themes

σὺν τοῖσδ' ἱκετῶν ἐγχειριδίοις
ἐριοστέπτοισι κλάδοισιν
With these wool-wreathed suppliants'
branches in our hands. (21-2)

Encheiridiois is denotatively adjectival in this passage, but as a substantive means "daggers." In like manner, the *mêchanê kalê* ("fair contrivance") to be resorted to if all else fails (459) might well signify to the audience—before the chorus continues to explain—the daggers of treachery. Nor could the phrase *eph' haimati* (6), descriptive of the crime of murder, fail to be suggestive. The murder may also be the point of reference of the Procne image in lines 58-67; the Danaids are probably here marked as *dusmatores* ("cruel mothers") who in killing their husbands, refuse the duties of motherhood, as Procne abandoned such duties by slaying her son. War between Egyptians and Argives is perhaps foreshadowed by remarks like that made by the herald in 950-1.[2] These predictions confirm nothing, however, not known to us from the passage in the *Prometheus* or from the Io allegory.

Much more can be learned from the choral benediction of Argos, which seems not to be an historical parabasis, but contains the interwoven threads of the more important themes of the *Suppliants* and the trilogy. So important is this stasimon that it warrants close attention here.

The first strophe (630-8) implores the gods to

[2] Cf. 634-8, 659-60, 678-83.

spare Argos from the destruction of war. Ares, characterized here as *machlos* ("lustful"), symbolizes not only war in general but specifically the Egyptians. This identification is completed by the use of the adjective *achoros*;[3] Ares is hostile to the dance, and so to the chorus itself. Reference to war and its devastation recur in strophe beta, ephymnion beta, strophe gamma, and strophe delta. In these passages the chorus thinks of the assault, both martial and sexual, of the Egyptians; their words, however, foreshadow the murder. In a sense, the Danaids are a "plague to men" (*loimos andrôn*, 659), and a "husband-slaying pestilence" (*androkmês loigos*, 678-9) as the Egyptians are a plague of men, the plague which can empty the *polis* of men, or a man-slaying pestilence. The Danaids are as great a danger to the state as are the Egyptians.

Antistrophe alpha voices a related theme central to the thought of the *Suppliants*. The Argives have offered protection to the Danaids because of the pollution which would otherwise have descended upon them. This pollution is represented by the image of a great bird befouling the rooftops.[4] Contrasted to the averted pollution is the freedom of the Argive altars from stain (654f) and the consequent good health, both religious and political, of the state (antistrophe beta, strophe and antistrophe delta). But again, the presence of the Danaids themselves is a real danger to those

[3] Cf. 681.
[4] The manuscript reading of lines 650-1 should surely stand. Cf. the similar metaphor in 751-2.

Hypermnestra and the Themes

same altars. They have threatened to pollute them figuratively and perhaps literally by murdering their husbands.

The significant theme of pollution occurs not only in the benediction of Argos, but in another passage sometimes said to owe its existence only to the poet's delight in narration, the story of the medicine-priest Apis (260-70). Pelasgus tells the chorus how Apis came to Argos and purified the land of "man-destroying monsters" (264), after the earth, polluted by bloodshed, had disgorged the creatures. How symbolic and prophetic this passage is! A new generation of man-destroying monsters, the Danaids (no less a *dusmenês ksunoikia*—"hateful colony"—than their prototypes) is to arise from the earth stained by the blood of their husbands; as Apis found eternal remembrance for the cure he effected (269-70), so will Hypermnestra and Lynceus for the purification they are to work by resolution of conflict.

Balancing the theme of war and pollution in the benediction of Argos is the praise of peace and the highest of its benefits, fertility, which is opposed to war's concomitants, death and sterility. The plea for peace is an ironic commentary on the Danaids' character. Not only do they destroy peace by their slaughter of the Egyptians, but in refusing motherhood they renounce fertility in favor of sterility. They assert,

> And we pray that a succession of guardians[5]
> of the land be born, and that Artemis Hecate
> watch over the child-bed of women. (674-7)

[5] Reading, with M, *d'ephorous*, which appears to make very

81

Hypermnestra and the Themes

but only Hypermnestra is fruitful like their ancestress Io. The continuing fertility of the descendants of the Zeus bull and Io cow is symbolically emphasized;

> And may the cattle grazing in the fields be prolific (691-2)

and the importance of reverence to parenthood is implied in the concluding words of the stasimon,

> For reverence for parents is written third among the statutes of Justice, who is honored above all. (707-9)

Hypermnestra alone observes this principal in deed; the other Danaids pay it only lip-service.

More informative still for the content of the lost plays is the exodos of the *Suppliants*. The chorus is divided into two factions;[6] the previously apparent unanimity is replaced by growing doubt in the minds of at least some of the maidens. The first semi-chorus (1018-33), which reiterates and develops the earlier thought of the Danaids, emphasizes again the incon-

---

good sense. It refers to the future guardians of Argos, the royal descendants of Hypermnestra.

[6] The frequently accepted theory that the maidservants are introduced as a second chorus in the exodos (cf. B. Todt, "Zur Erklärung und Kritik von Aeschylos' Schutzflehenden," *Philologus*, 48 [1889], pp. 50-6) is based on highly controversial evidence. The *opadoi* of 1022 can better refer back to the armed attendants of 954 (cf. Sophocles, *Trachiniae*, 1264) than the *dmôides* of 977. *Hypodeksasthe* (1022) does not mean "take up," but "give ear to" or "listen to" (cf. Hesiod, *Theogony*, 419; Herodotus 8.106). See C. Van der Graaf, "Les Suivantes dans la Choeur Finale des Suppliantes d'Eschyle," *Mnemosyne* 10 (1942), pp. 281-5.

sistency of their understanding of the relationship of their situation to the story of Io. In effect, they renounce further comparison with Io;

> No longer let us honor in our song the flowing outlets of the Nile (1024-5)

and turn to the worship of

> the rivers that pour their kindly draught through the land and bring increase of children (1026-8).

Curiously, in the face of this renunciation, the rivers of Argos (and we think again of Inachus and the fruitful Io) are marked as *polyteknoi* ("with many children");[7] yet the maidens immediately contradict the thread of their thought by appealing to the chaste goddess Artemis (1030-1). These words are the expression of the confused, blinded mental processes of those sisters who murder their husbands, who can reach to no truly deep understanding of the meaning of the legend of Io and Zeus. The second semi-chorus (1034-51) strongly suggests the gathering doubt—or rather, increasing understanding—which culminated in the positive action of one of their number, Hypermnestra. The power of Aphrodite is not forgotten, and specifically her vital role in marriage (1035);[8] she is conceded to be a more powerful deity than Artemis,

[7] The Freudian critic would undoubtedly find obvious sex symbolism in the very frequent reference to rivers (the lifegiving Nile, Inachus, etc.).
[8] Cf. Wilamowitz, *op. cit.*, p. 22.

Hypermnestra and the Themes

invoked by the first semi-chorus. The emphasis on desire and persuasion as components of Aphrodite's powers (1039-40) foreshadows the emergence of Hypermnestra as a personality distinct from her sisters. In the antistrophe, the semi-chorus expresses a resigned, almost fatalistic attitude in foreboding of marriage with the Egyptians, admitting the possibility that Zeus himself may not oppose this union,

> that which is fated shall come to pass. The mighty, boundless mind of Zeus cannot be transgressed. (1047-9)

and even suggesting that marriage, as woman's allotted fate, should be the fate of the sisters themselves,

> may marriage be our destiny, as it has been the destiny of many women before us. (1050-1)

The subsequent choral exchange debates the validity of this idea, as that part of the chorus which symbolizes Hypermnestra's rebellion seeks to moderate the violence and bias of the other sisters.[9] The full chorus then concludes the drama with the ambiguous application of the Io imagery discussed above.[10] The final appeal of the maidens, expressed in broad, indefinite terms, is most significant:

> And may he [Zeus] award victory to the women. I shall be content with that which is

[9] Mazon's distribution of these lines (1052-61) seems more intelligible than Murray's.
[10] Cf. above, pp. 66-7.

Hypermnestra and the Themes

> better than evil, even though it be mixed,
> and content that justice follow upon justice,
> in accordance with my prayers, through the
> redeeming ways of God. (1068-73)

Each of these thoughts is prophetic. The Danaids, in words somewhat less extreme than those of the first semi-chorus, plead for victory for the women; they are indeed triumphant when they murder their husbands, but Hypermnestra wins a bloodless and more glorious victory. Later events are "better than evil" only because they are mitigated by Hypermnestra's action. True justice (the sparing of Lynceus and the subsequent acquittal of Hypermnestra) supersedes the apparent but superficial justice of the death of the Egyptians; this true justice is effected by "the redeeming ways of God" as Zeus, through the agency of Aphrodite, justifies the deeds of Hypermnestra, his genuine "daughter" by Io.

It is, of course, impossible to reconstruct in any detail the elements of later action foreshadowed in the *Suppliants*. In all likelihood, however, the second play terminated in the marriage and apparent triumph of the Egyptians, as the *Suppliants* ends with the seeming victory of the Danaids. The final play, then, portrayed resolution after thesis and antithesis; this is the structural principle of the *Oresteia*. We must, I believe, assume that Hypermnestra, not the guilty sisters, was brought to trial in the *Danaids*; she must have emerged, by this time, as the principal character of the trilogy, and a mass trial of the Danaids would result only in loss of effective dramatic focus.[11] Aphrodite's defense of Hypermnestra must logically have insisted on the power of love and the importance for humanity of marriage and fertility; these theses are inherent in the Io allegory and thoroughly consonant with fragment 44. Since the fate of the guilty maidens could not be altogether ignored, the goddess may have enjoined, as a fit punishment, their enforced marriage to competitors in a foot race;[12] such a device would not merely permit the poet to bind loose dramatic threads, but would serve to emphasize further the virtue and wisdom of Hypermnestra, the focal figure of the trilogy.

For ultimately it is Hypermnestra, the new Io, who resolves the problems posed in the trilogy, although she must be assisted by the divine wisdom and guidance. War and sterility, destroyers of men and cities and polluters of altars, are embraced by her sisters, who choose a personal—and deceptive—good; Hypermnestra, through her choice of the blessings of peace and fertility, reconciles the good of God, community, and individual. Like Io, she assures the perpetuation of man and his nobility, the legacies of the tormented *Prometheus*. In her choice, and in her ability to choose, lie the essence of the Danaid myth as shaped by the art of Aeschylus; man, through the proper exercise

[11] It is conceivable that the *Danaids* contained no trial at all. We are perhaps unduly influenced by the example of the *Eumenides*; the appearance of Aphrodite may merely have interrupted the intended punishment of Hypermnestra by her father.

[12] Cf. above, p. 13 and Ch. I, note 30.

Hypermnestra and the Themes

of wisdom and understanding (which will reveal to him the necessity of co-operation with the divine intent and of remaining true to his own fundamental nature) may transmute apparent evil into tangible and enduring good.

These human implications emerge against a background of cosmic harmony not unlike the metaphysical beliefs of pre-Socratic philosophy. In a sense, the love of Zeus for Io is the love of heaven for earth, the principle binding in concord the antagonistic elements of the universe:

> The holy heaven longs to wound the earth, and desire grips the earth for marriage: the rain falling from heaven in his marriage-bed impregnates the earth; she brings forth for mortals the food of flocks and Demeter's fruits. And from this damp wedding the trees come into flower at their fixed season. Of all these things I am in part the cause.
> (fr. 44)

The marriage of Lynceus and Hypermnestra is the realization in human terms of these benign powers of the cosmos.

APPENDIX A

The Chronology of the *Suppliants* and the *Prometheus Bound*

It is not my intention, in this brief discussion, to advance a new theory of the date of the *Suppliants*, nor to debate the findings of scholars who have examined, in great detail, the evidence for the dating of the *Prometheus*. My contention is simply that no evidence, external or internal, excludes the possibility that the composition of the *Prometheus* was approximately contemporary with that of the *Suppliants*, and that good evidence points to the probability of such contemporaneity (cf. above, pp. 48-55).

In the case of the *Prometheus*, a *terminus post quem* is fairly well established by the poet's apparent reference to the eruption of Etna (lines 363-72); the tragedy was very probably written after 479/8, and some scholars even refer it to the last years of the poet's career.[1] Evidence for the date of the *Suppliants* has been, until recently, more dubious. The publication of the papyrus which indicates that the Danaid trilogy was produced in competition with plays of Sophocles,

[1] Cf. W. B. Stanford, *Aeschylus in his Style*, p. 138. The more conventional view is typified by Friedrich Focke, "Aischylos' Prometheus," *Hermes* 65 (1930), p. 263. Focke believes the play was written in about 470.

Appendix A

now suggests that the trilogy was presented in the late 460's.[2] This new evidence counters the traditional belief, founded on exceedingly tenuous grounds, that the *Suppliants* is a very early play, belonging possibly to the 490's.

Previous attempts to date the *Suppliants* fall largely into two categories; stylistic analysis, and speculation concerning certain "political references" in the play. Neither approach has proved ultimately fruitful. Much of the earlier stylistic analysis was vitiated by the fact that its users set out to prove what they already "knew" —i.e., that the *Suppliants* is an early play.[3] Thus the preponderance of the choral element proves that the drama marks a primitive stage in the development of tragedy out of the purely choral dithyramb.[4] This in face of the quantitative and qualitative importance of the choral element of the *Oresteia*! The bulk of such criticism seems similarly tautological.[5]

[2] *Pap. Oxy.* 2256.3. See the thorough discussion by A. Lesky, "Die Datierung der Hiketiden und der Tragiker Mesatos," *Hermes* 82 (1954), pp. 1-13.

[3] Both W. B. Stanford (*Aeschylus in his Style*) and F. R. Earp (*The Style of Aeschylus*, Cambridge, 1940) err in this respect; Stanford in lesser degree.

[4] Cf. N. Wecklein, review of Mueller's *de Aeschyli Supplicum Tempore atque Indole*, *Berliner Philologische Wochenschrift* 30 (1910), cols. 737-9.

[5] It is true, of course, that the *Suppliants* and the *Prometheus* are not, in general, similar in style; the language of the former is complex and difficult, while the style of the *Prometheus* is comparatively clear and direct. I attribute this difference to Aeschylus' artistry in adapting style to subject matter and intent. The *Prometheus* is a play of prophecy, of the Forethinker's rationality set against despotic force; the focus of the *Suppliants* is on the irrational aberrations of the Danaids.

Appendix A

The historical approach has met with no greater success. Political allusions in the play have been related to conditions in Greece from 495/4 down to 470.[6] It is now equally logical to assume that the *Suppliants* is historically appropriate in the 460's. The marked interest in Egypt, and in relations between Egypt and Argos, may indeed reflect the growing awareness of the importance of Egypt during the period of the insurrection of Inaros. Surely the "Egyptian question" must have been hotly debated in Athens at that time, and Aeschylus may well have wished to make dramatic capital of the new interest. It is even tempting to suppose that Inaros might have supported his appeal for Athenian aid by reference to a mythical racial kinship (it was a commonplace among the Greeks that their ancestry could be traced to Egypt).[7] This is, of course, speculation; the important point is that the *Suppliants* is as much at home in the political scene of the middle or late 460's as in any other period, and more so than in some.

In each case, the language is fully appropriate. Further, it should be noted that the monologues of the maddened Io in the *Prometheus* are stylistically as turbid as comparable passages in the *Suppliants*.

[6] For example, B. Lavagnini, "Per la cronologia delle Supplici di Eschilo," *Rivista di Filologia e di Istruzione Classica* 60 (1932), pp. 369-71, dates the *Suppliants* in the late 90's. But Otto Könnecke, in a review of F. Helmreich's *Der Chor im Drama des Aeschylus*, in *Wochenschrift für Klassische Philologie*, 33 (1916), col. 387, using the same evidence, dates the play in 462!

[7] Might there not have been, during the early years of the insurrection, some interesting confusion in Athens between a corruption of the name Inarus and the Argive Inachus?

Appendix A

Although stylistic and historical criteria afford little sound evidence for the early dating of the play, certain scholars have undertaken to prove that the *Suppliants* and the *Prometheus* cannot be assigned to the same period of the poet's career. They base their arguments on differences in the description of the physical appearance of Io and discrepancies in the treatment of her story in the two plays. Such contentions are founded on the dubious assumption that the selective process of the artist, and his aesthetic intent, cannot differ from year to year or day to day. If it can be shown that these differences were dictated by the poet's varied aims, then one must conclude that they afford no chronological evidence whatsoever.

In the *Suppliants* Io is referred to as either a cow (lines 17, 44, 170, 275, and 299-314) or, in one instance only, as part human, part cow (*boton . . . meiksombroton*, 568). These references are advanced by Korte as evidence that the *Suppliants* was written at a time when the old theriomorphic tradition was still in full sway.[8] On the other hand, Io in the *Prometheus* is never referred to as a cow, but either as a maiden (589, 608) or as a horned maiden (588, 674). Korte concludes that the portrayal of the *Prometheus* represents a literary departure from theriomorphism that was accompanied by a similar change in the visual arts;[9] J. C. Hoppin holds that this change,

[8] "Die Entstehungszeit der Hiketiden des Aischylos," *Mélanges Nicole*, pp. 290-1.
[9] *Ibid.* This innovation in representations of Io on red-figured vases is incontestable.

Appendix A

which occurred about 470, was occasioned by the example furnished by the *Prometheus*.[10]

Several flaws can be detected in such reasoning. First, these scholars overlooked the fact that the role of Io is totally different in the two tragedies; in the *Suppliants*, she is merely invoked, while in the *Prometheus* she appears onstage as *dramatis persona*. Surely we could not expect the poet to violate the tragic dignity by allowing the presence onstage of some absurd cow-like contrivance.[11] The simplest and most logical solution for the dramatist was the portrayal of Io as a horned maiden; obviously, then, she cannot be referred to as *bous*, but must be addressed as "horned maiden" (*parthenos boukerôs*). In the *Suppliants*, however, the full atmosphere of the old myth can be preserved, and Io must be thought of as in cow form in order to make fully meaningful the bull-cow image.

Korte's theory is open to a second serious objection; the occurrence of the word *meiksombrotos* in the *Suppliants* (568) casts considerable doubt on the "total theriomorphism" of the play, since it indicates that Io, in the mind of poet and chorus, retained a degree (indeterminate) of her human physical characteristics. One scholar even asserts that the word must refer in *retrospect* to the *Prometheus*, or to some other lost

[10] "Argos, Io, and the Prometheus of Aeschylus," *Harvard Studies in Classical Philology* 12 (1901), pp. 335-45.

[11] Cf. Eitrem, *Real-Encyclopädie*, 9^2, s.v. Io; Roscher, *Lexicon*, vol. 2, col. 271. Oceanus, who appears in the *Prometheus* on his four-legged bird, is intended to be sententiously comic; Io is always pathetic or tragic.

Appendix A

tragedy which had abandoned the theriomorphic portrayal of Io.[12]

Evidence so patently debatable has not much weight. We can only assume that Aeschylus' decision to follow the legend somewhat more literally in the *Suppliants* was dictated by his poetic purpose; his decision to depict Io as a horned maiden in the *Prometheus* was necessitated by the requirements of the theater. Had he written the latter play at the beginning of his career, and the former at the end, he would have been confronted with the same choice, and his decisions would have been the same.[13]

It is further objected that the accounts of Io's affair with Zeus, and of her wanderings, differ in the *Suppliants* and the *Prometheus*.[14] In the *Prometheus*, for example, Io apparently (according to her own words) remains a virgin until she reaches Egypt, while in the *Suppliants* Zeus forces his attentions on her in Argos. The enmity of Hera is also less emphasized in the *Prometheus* than in the *Suppliants*. This discrepancy can, perhaps, be explained in part as a skillful stroke of characterization; the shy and deeply-shamed maiden cannot, as she tells her story, dwell on such episodes and still remain in character. More important, Aeschylus' dramatic purpose prevented him from following

---

[12] Roscher, *loc. cit.*

[13] It should be noted that the literary portrayal of Io as a cow did not disappear in later centuries. Cf. *A. P.* 7.169; Propertius 2.28.18; Ovid, *Metam.* 1.610-14.

[14] Cf. Korte, *op. cit.*; Walther Kranz, *Stasimon* (Berlin 1933), p. 107; Vürtheim, *op. cit.*, pp. 37-8.

Appendix A

the same account in both plays. Io's story in the *Prometheus* exposes Zeus to a more serious charge than does the account of the affair in the *Suppliants*. It reveals a crafty, planned campaign by the mightiest of gods. Dreams and the authority of oracles are employed to seduce the virtuous maiden (645-72), while early and easier submission to the lust of Zeus would withdraw our sympathy from Io, and lessen our antipathy to the willful character of the Olympian. The subservient Apollo forces Io's father, under threat of destruction of his *genos*, to turn her out of the palace and banish her from her homeland:

> to thrust me forth from home and fatherland, to wander at large [*apheton*] to earth's remotest boundaries (665-6).

A forceful ambiguity in these lines emphasizes the scheming of the god. Io is to be "let loose" (*apheton*). This word is also used of animals dedicated to a god; thus Io's role is that of a sacrificial animal in the *Prometheus*, where the poet wishes to underline the primitive cruelty of Zeus; in the *Suppliants*, where the chorus is primarily conscious of the developed deity who released Io, Zeus's role in the affair is treated more sympathetically.

A more serious discrepancy, which may appear to evidence outright contradiction rather than selection, occurs between the account of the conception of Epaphus by the touch and on-breathing of Zeus in the *Suppliants*, and the prediction made by Prometheus,

Appendix A

> There at length Zeus shall restore your reason by the caress [*epaphôn*] of his unterrifying hand and his touch alone. (848-9)

Vürtheim concludes that these lines are clearly a reference to the "older" version of the story told in the *Suppliants*, because the poet informs us here that the conception was the result of *thiksis* alone, not of *thiksis* and *epipnoia*; he insists that Aeschylus unequivocally shows us that the *Suppliants* preceded the *Prometheus*.[15] Yet what truly plausible explanation can be furnished for the poet's decision to omit the story of the *epipnoia*, and to draw attention to the fact, in the later version, that he has omitted it? My conclusion is that these lines have been misinterpreted. Prometheus has completed his recitation of the torments caused Io by the lust of the cruel deity; now he tells her of her reward for those labors. He informs her that she will end her long journey in Egypt, will give birth to the glorious Epaphus, and thus found a mighty line of ruling heroes. What, then, could be more fitting than for Prometheus to make clear to her that the conception of Epaphus will not result from enforced sexual possession by Zeus, but from the touch of his hand alone? In other words, the adverb *monon* does not exclude the concept of *epipnoia*, but only that of physical sexual intercourse; it merely emphasizes the gentleness of Io's lover when the discipline of destiny has run its full course. Consequently, these lines, if they afford any evidence at all for the comparative chronology of

[15] *Op. cit.*, p. 37.

Appendix A

the plays, might be used to support the view that the *Suppliants* followed the *Prometheus*, and that Aeschylus chose to add to the *Suppliants* the theme of *epipnoia* as the nucleus of the imagery of breath, wind, and storm.

Korte holds that the simpler treatment of the story of Io's wanderings in the *Suppliants* is evidence that the play is earlier than the *Prometheus*, with its detailed, imaginative geographical account.[16] This assumption is surely based on misunderstanding of the function of the accounts of Io's travels in each drama. In the *Suppliants*, a brief, concise story of Io's wanderings is necessary to assist in the establishment of kinship between the Danaids and their ancestress, while a lengthier description would merely divert the attention of the audience from the central dramatic problem. In the *Prometheus*, the extended account serves to emphasize the immensity of Io's travail, and thus to characterize further the violence and cruelty of the new Olympian regime. In addition, the storied travels to strange and distant lands assist in intensifying the play's atmosphere of mystery and wonder, and help in stressing the cosmic nature of the problems involved. Vürtheim rightly observes that the description of Io's travels in the *Suppliants* differs from that of the *Prometheus* because it is governed by different poetic and dramatic demands.[17]

There are other, less important, discrepancies in

[16] *Op. cit.*, pp. 291-2.
[17] *Op. cit.*, p. 53.

Appendix A

the two accounts which need not detain us.[18] The Danaid myth was old and varied: Aeschylus was under no compulsion to select one version and to reproduce it in all meticulous detail each time he used the story. Moreover, his artistic intent was the same in no two plays—if variations in detail served his immediate purpose, he was perfectly free to alter or adapt his earlier account. In summary, it seems apparent that the comparison of the treatment of the Io myth in the *Suppliants* and *Prometheus* affords no more substantial evidence for the dating of either play than does stylistic analysis, and examination of historical allusion in the case of the former; none of these methods of scholarship renders impossible or even unlikely the chronological proximity of the two tragedies.

[18] For these minor discrepancies, see G. Mueller, *De Aeschyli Supplicum Tempore atque Indole* (Halle, 1908).

APPENDIX B

Line 8 and the Motivation of the Danaids

The manuscript reading for this crucial line is ἀλλ' αὐτογένητον φυλαξάνοραν, with λα *in rasura* and γρ. φυξάνοραν written in the margin. Most editors have rejected the peculiar compound *phylaksanoran* as a corrector's conjecture. In the majority of editions, Bamberger's emendation αὐτογενεῖ φυξανορίᾳ has been accepted without change, despite its assumption that the copyist gratuitously added the letters *-ton*, and even though it created a curious *hapax legomenon* in *phyksanoria*. Wilamowitz translates this emended reading as "angeborene männerfeindschaft"[1] and employs it as an element in his argument that the Danaids exhibit Amazon-like characteristics, and shun all marriage. *Autogenês* does not, however, mean "inborn"; in every attested occurrence, it signifies "self-produced." Emendation of the line is clearly necessary, but Bamberger's reading appears inadequate.

A more likely solution which, unlike Bamberger's emendation, requires no change in the word *autogenêton* (which does not evidence traces of erasure or correction) is the reading ἀλλ' αὐτογενῆ τὸν φύλακ' ἀνδρῶν.[2]

[1] *Op. cit.*, p. 15.
[2] Lack of diaeresis after the second metron rules against the ms. *autogenêton*.

Appendix B

The key word *phylak'* is thoroughly consistent with the patterns of the play's imagery. In 303, the chorus relates of Argus that

τὸν πάνθ' ὁρῶντα φύλακ' ἐπέστησεν βοΐ

and in 382-3, the chorus prays to Zeus as *phylaka polyponôn brotôn*. Further, Danaus warns his daughters that virginity is difficult to guard:

τέρειν' ὀπώρα δ' εὐφύλακτος οὐδαμῶς· (998)

The relevance and intent of the image seem clear. Argus was Io's *phylaks* ("keeper," "guard"), and the Egyptians a would-be *phylaks*, whom the Danaids abhor as their ancestress did Argus. Yet, once more, the maidens' comprehension is not deep, for they pray to Zeus to undertake the same role, forgetting the full and ironic implications of their request. Finally, virginity is not easily guarded, says Danaus, with overtones suggesting the death of Argus, his own (Danaus') defeat and submission to the Egyptians, and eventually the consummation of Hypermnestra's marriage with Lynceus. It is also worth noting that forms of *phylaks* and *phylattô* occur twelve times in the *Suppliants*, as against an average of three times in the six other plays. This fact alone indicates that the root and idea of words suggesting the range of connotation "protector-custodian-jailer" were attractive to Aeschylus in the structure of the play. We should, therefore, be most reluctant to emend out of existence another occurrence of an apparent root of a word belonging to this family.

In further explanation of the possible meaning of

Appendix B

this passage it seems clear that *autogenês* must be constructed with the phrase contained in 8-10, and not with the preceding clause. Its proximity to *gamon* is paralleled by *Prometheus* 855-6, where the marriage of Danaids and Egyptians is described as *syngenê gamon anepsiôn*.[3] In this passage we may find a clue to the meaning of *autogenês*.

One might conclude, on first impression, that the poet used *syngenês* and *autogenês* as synonyms, with prefix altered for metrical considerations only. Close inspection of Aeschylean and typical Greek usage shows this, however, to be improbable. *Syngenês* is commonly used to denote kinship, while *autogenês* and *autogenêtos* mean "self-produced." *Auto-* and *syn-*, moreover, do not possess the same force as prefixes, but the substitution of one for the other frequently changes altogether the meaning of a compound; cf. *autoboulos* vs. *symboulos*, *autotelês* vs. *syntelês*. Possibly Aeschylus' use of *autogenês* in line 8 was a conscious attempt at *paraprosdokian*, especially if he had previously written *Prometheus* 855.

If taken, then, with the clause contained in 8-10, *autogenês* cannot refer to the Danaids, but must signify some attribute or activity of the Egyptians: it is a marriage which would occur only because the males desire it; for the Danaids to accept them would be for them to accept a "self-produced jailer." It would not be, as they feel it should be, a marriage created by mutual desire and consent. Lines 8-10 may then be literally translated:

[3] Cf. also *Prom.* 14, 39, and 289.

Appendix B

But abhorring as self-produced "the watcher of men," and marriage with the sons of Aegyptus as unholy.

The construction *phylak' andrôn* may literally mean "a guardian of (for) men," and might suggest that the motive of the Egyptians is to be found in their desire to perpetuate their house by offspring from a marriage with the Danaids. Probably there is, however, at least a strong connotative sense of hatred of the Egyptians as a "jailer" consisting of males.[4] Such a meaning would be thoroughly consonant with the Danaids' ambiguous attitude toward the story of Io. The image refers, at the moment, to the afflicted Io unwillingly constrained by the jailer Argus, but less patently (and beyond their vision) to Zeus, and eventually to Lynceus, as the benevolent *phylakes* (now "protectors") of their race.

In conclusion, it seems that, in the present state of our knowledge, line 8 offers no evidence of a general misanthropy as the motive for the Danaids' resistance to marriage with the Egyptians.[5] In contrast, if the reading *phylak' andrôn* should be correct, the passage tends to confirm the view that the maidens abhor their

[4] Construing *andrôn* as "genitive of material"; cf. *herkos odontôn*, and the ambiguous construction of *andrôn* in line 659.

[5] Nor does it lend aid to Hiltbrunner's theory (*op. cit.*) that they regard the right to virginity as a prerogative (*timê*) established in their line by Zeus's miraculous begetting of Epaphus. His theory, while not unattractive, is largely supported by such evidence as that of the dubious line 8, and is vitiated by an apparent underestimation of the importance of the role of Danaus, who is, after all, regarded by the maidens as their leader (*boularchos* and *stasiarchos*, 11-12).

Appendix B

cousins because of the unconcealed violence of the Egyptians, a violence perhaps resulting in part from the failure of the Danaids to reciprocate the men's affections.[6] The brutality of the Egyptians, stressed not only by the Danaids, but by their own vicious actions on stage and by the reactions of Pelasgus, is surely a simple and sufficient motive for the maidens' reluctance to submit to such suitors.

[6] For a parallel to this feminine reaction to a marriage of constraint, see Euripides, *Medea*, 232-40, where the husband is described as *despotên sômatos*. Aeschylus is not a social critic in the Euripidean sense, but it is manifest that he was not unaware of the plight of the woman in an unhappy marriage. Cf. his apparent sympathy for Clytemnestra (insofar as she has genuinely been wronged by Agamemnon).